…"No one can safely pass
That fateful wheel. Who has by wisdom or
By manliness escaped the knife-sharp claws
Of that celestial dragon? What has to be
Will be. There is no doubt. The shrewdest man
Has not escaped his fate."…

In the Dragon's *Claws*

**THE STORY OF ROSTAM & ESFANDIYAR
FROM THE PERSIAN BOOK OF KINGS
BY ABOLQASEM FERDOWSI**

Translated *&* Introduced
by Jerome W. Clinton

MAGE PUBLISHERS
WASHINGTON, DC

Designed by Mage Publishers

Jacket and title page is a *Shahnameh* lithograph of
Rostam (Tahamtan) slaying Esfandiyār
by Mirza 'Ali-Qoli Khu'i (edition Teheran 1265-67),
kindly supplied from the archive of lithograph book illustration
by Dr. Ulrich Marzolph, Goettingen, Germany

LIBRARY OF CONGRESS CATALOGING-IN-PUBLICATION DATA
Firdawsi.
   [Rustam va Isfandiyar. English]
   In the dragon's claws: the story of Rostam & Esfandiyar, from
the Persian Book of kings by Abolqasem Ferdowsi / translated,
introduced, and annotated by Jerome W. Clinton
   p.   cm.
   Includes bibliographical references (p.).
   ISBN 0-934211-55-8 (pbk.: alk. paper)
   I. Clinton, Jerome W. II. Title.
PK6456.A12R82   1999
891'.5511--DC21   98-32324 CIP

FIRST EDITION
PRINTED AND MANUFACTURED
IN THE UNITED STATES OF AMERICA

Mage books are available at bookstores or directly from the publisher.
To receive our latest catalog, call toll free 1-800-962-0922
or visit Mage online at www.mage.com.

For Asha,
healer of my soul,
love of my life

Table of Contents

Introduction 9

The Family of Goshtāsp 24

The Family of Rostam 26

Geography 27

In the Dragon's Claws 29

Further Reading 139

ACKNOWLEDGMENTS

The preparation of this translation was made possible in part by a grant from the National Endowment for the Humanities, an independent federal agency, whose assistance I gratefully acknowledge.

I would like to thank here my friends and colleagues Robert Fagles, Charles P. Melville, Suleiman Grosslight, Stephen Dale and Jocelyn Sharlet who kindly read the manuscript at different stages, and helped me with their comments and encouragement. I owe a special debt of thanks to my friend and colleague, Dick Davis, who read the whole of the final draft and made many helpful suggestions.

I would also like to thank professors Ja'far She'ar and Hasan Anvari, whose copiously annotated edition of the *Razmnāmeh-ye Rostam va Esfandiyār* time and again clarified what was obscure and smoothed the way before me.

Introduction: The Shahnameh

The story of Rostam and Esfandiyār is taken from the *Shahnameh*, or *Book of Kings*, a long narrative poem in Persian that was given its present form by Abolqasem Ferdowsi (AD 932–1025). The many heroic tales that fill the *Shahnameh* (Book of kings) are drawn from the history and mythology of Iran, and some of them at least were recited at the courts of Cyrus and Darius in the sixth century BC. In the course of the centuries that followed, these epic tales were gathered together into a book from time to time, but none of these earlier collections has survived. In the tenth century, one such recension, in prose, came into the hands of Ferdowsi, a minor noble who lived in the city of Tus near present-day Mashhad. Although Ferdowsi was a Muslim, he was devoted to the ancient traditions of Iran and feared that they would be lost as Islamic culture became ever more deeply rooted in Iran. To help forestall this, he set himself the task of retelling all the tales of the *Shahnameh* in poetry so that they would be remembered and passed on. The labor took him thirty-five years, but the result was a masterly work, nearly 50,000 couplets in length, that has enjoyed enormous popularity throughout the Persian speaking world for a millennium. It was discovered by European scholars in the eighteenth century and eventually translated into all the major languages of Europe.

Ferdowsi also assumed that in giving poetic life to these

tales he would assure the survival of his own name as well.

> When this my famous book shall reach its end,
> My praises will be heard throughout the land.
> From this day on I shall not die, but live,
> For I'll have sown my words both far and wide.

In this he was successful beyond his wildest dreams. No name resonates more powerfully in the history of Iranian culture than that of its greatest poet, Abolqasem Ferdowsi.

In its length and its concentration on heroic action the *Shahnameh* resembles the western epic tradition, but in other important respects it differs substantially from Homer, Virgil and their imitators. It begins, for instance, not "in the midst of things" as does the *Iliad*, but with the creation of the world and the appearance of the first shah. The many and varied stories that make up the *Shahnameh* are joined together not by the force of a single hero like Odysseus, nor by the movement toward a single climactic event, such as the fall of Troy, but by the dynastic history of the Iranian court. This long and vivid history ends when that sequence of rulers does; that is, with the Arab, Islamic invasion of the seventh century AD that replaced the Iranian shahanshah ("emperor") with an Islamic caliph.

Since the focus of the tales is the life of the royal court, one finds little mention in the *Shahnameh* of the life of ordinary people such as farmers, shepherds or craftsmen. In this it resembles Malory's tales of King Arthur and the knights of the round table more than it does Homer or Virgil. As in the court of Arthur as well, a single god, called Izad or Yazdān, rules over the universe of the *Shahnameh*, not the celestial college of the Greeks and Romans. The horse riding *pahlavāns* ("heroes") of the Persian court battle each other using lances, shields and heavy maces much as did the knights of King Arthur's round table.

The events of the Shahnameh stretch across many generations and so are not tailored to the life span of a single hero. However, the principal figures in its dramas live as long as Biblical patriarchs, and one in particular, Rostam, endures for nearly nine centuries. Rostam is the last and greatest of a family of heroes from the Iranian province of Sistān, and he is a central presence in several of its finest stories. His death, which takes place just after the events of the present tale, and as a result of them, concludes the purely legendary portion of the *Shahnameh*. In the last third, the tales are peopled with figures from historical times. One portion draws heavily on a fictional biography of Alexander the Great, who conquered all of present-day Iran and parts of Central Asia and North India in the fourth century BC. The last sequence of stories is a similarly fictionalized account of the history of the Parthian and Sasanian dynasties (247 BC–AD651) who ruled in Iran between the time of Alexander's death and the rise of Islam. The style of presentation does not change; however, historical figures and events are presented as the stuff of myth and legend.

In the world of the *Shahnameh*, humankind seems to have existed before the first shah but as an undifferentiated species. The formation of human society required the shaping presence of a divinely appointed ruler. Other shahs, most notably Hushang and Jamshid, the Iranian Solomon, provided human society with those gifts—fire, tools, agriculture and the various crafts—that raise men and women above the level of beasts. In other traditions these gifts that distinguish and sustain human society are gifts from the gods. In the *Shahnameh* it is Iran's shahs who provide them, or, rather, it is through them that

Yazdān, the sole god of pre-Islamic Iranian religious belief, gives them to mankind.

While there are a number of recurrent themes in the *Shahnameh*, such as the immortality of noble deeds, the malignancy and inevitability of fate, and the persistent hostility and envy of Iran's neighbors, the theme that underlies all of these is that God prefers Iran to other nations and sustains it through the institution of the shah. So long as His chosen shah sits upon the throne, Iran will endure. When Shah Yazdegerd III is slain in AD 652, the Iran of the *Shahnameh* comes to an end. Other epics use a single dominant hero, like Odysseus, Aeneas or Roland, or a single, epochal event—the destruction of Troy, the founding of Rome or the defeat of the Saracens—to provide dramatic unity. In the *Shahnameh* it is the enduring institution of monarchy that stitches all its stories together.

Although the Divinity's support for Iranian monarchy is a central constant of the *Shahnameh*, its ideology is not a naïve and enthusiastic monarchism. Ferdowsi was not a panegyrist who presented idealizations of the ruler for the admiration of the royal sponsors and their followers. He was as realistic about the limitations of individual monarchs as was Shakespeare. Many of the greatest tales in the epic, like *Rostam and Esfandiyār*, explore the terrible consequences that result when a bad or foolish shah sits upon the throne.

THE PERSIAN LANGUAGE

Persian belongs to the Indo-European family of languages and has strong similarities to the major languages of Europe—the words for father, mother and brother, for instance, are *pedar, mādar* and *barādar*. Old Persian, one of the court languages of Cyrus and Darius, was a contemporary of Sanskrit and closely resembled it. Middle Persian languages had wide currency in Central Asia and the Iranian plateau from the time of Alexander in the fourth century BC to the rise of Islam in the seventh century AD. Modern Persian evolved in the Islamic period from these Middle Persian languages. Its grammar and syntax is Persian, but it contains a large vocabulary of Arabic. The *Shahnameh* is written in a slightly archaized form of this language that is virtually free of Arabic loanwords. Since the ninth century Modern Persian has been written in a modified form of the Arabic alphabet.

Persian and Persian literature first came to the West as a result of the European conquest of India. For centuries Central Asian Muslims, whose literary and administrative language was Persian, ruled in India. When European merchants and adventurers became interested in India in the seventeenth century, they learned Persian in order to trade and rule. Then as now the principal texts for teaching the language were literary, and many of those who learned Persian for practical reasons came to value it as a source of pleasure and a focus of scholarship. One of the principal fruits of this scholarship was the "discovery" of the *Shahnameh*, or *Book of Kings* and its translation into the major languages of Europe. In the nineteenth century the English rulers replaced Persian with English as the language of education and administration in India, but Persian continued as a major language there until well into the twentieth century.

THE STORY OF ROSTAM AND ESFANDIYĀR
For a work that is usually described as one of the greatest stories of the Iranian national epic, the story of Rostam and Esfandiyār displays a surprisingly modern skepticism about the values we associate with the epic. In the world of the *Shahnameh*, monarchy enjoys divine sanction and society's most admired virtues

are embodied in heroes like Rostam and Esfandiyār, yet the story expresses a profound ambivalence about the demands of heroism and is sharply critical of a monarch who exploits the courage and loyalty of his heroes to further his own selfish ends. The climactic event of the story is the battle between Rostam and Esfandiyār, yet the two heroes do not view themselves as natural enemies. On the contrary, they fight each other against their own wishes and in violation of their own best interests. Moreover, theirs is a battle in which the roles of victor and vanquished seem to have been reversed. Although it is Esfandiyār who dies, the outcome is as tragic for the ancient hero as it is for the young prince. Esfandiyār loses his life and fails in his ambition to rule Iran as a consequence, but he dies with his reputation unsullied and confident that his actions in this world will be judged favorably by God in the next. Rostam gains only a brief respite from defeat and death, and does so at the cost of enduring shame for having slain the only Iranian hero whose virtues and accomplishments approach his own. The one person who may be said to gain by this tragedy, Shah Goshtāsp, pays a heavy price for his triumph as well. The defeat and death of his son lets him sit more easily on his throne, but as a result of it he loses the esteem of his own people, alienates his courtiers and brings disgrace on his family. His victory is a pyrrhic one.

While the narrative focus of the story is the slowly escalating tension between Esfandiyār and Rostam, a tension that explodes in their final tragic confrontation, the engine that drives their struggle is the conflict between Esfandiyār and his father over which of them will rule Iran. The seed of that conflict is in the shah's inability to understand and value his son, not in any failure of loyalty on his son's part. However, it is the son who will suffer the consequences of this, not the father.

As a young man, Goshtāsp was so resentful of his father's reluctance to abdicate in his favor that he was willing to lead the army of Iran's enemy to the west, Rome (Byzantium), against him. When Esfandiyār as a young prince distinguishes himself in a battle against Arjāsp, the ruler of Turān, Iran's hostile neighbor to the north, and so wins the loyalty and admiration of the army, Goshtāsp assumes that his son is as ambitious for rule as he himself was. When an envious courtier, Gorazm, accuses Esfandiyār of plotting against the shah, Goshtāsp believes him and has his son thrown in prison despite his plea that he is innocent. The irony in this is that Esfandiyār is cut from another pattern than the shah, and more nearly resembles his loyal and heroic uncle, Zarir, with whom he is often compared. Initially, at least, he is animated by simple loyalty and virtue, and does not covet his father's throne. Goshtāsp cannot see this and so abandons him to the prison fortress of Gombadān, and rides off to Zābolestān for a long visit with Rostam.

When Arjāsp and his ally, the Khāqān of China, learn that the shah has left his capital and that Iran's greatest hero is in prison, they launch a second invasion and quickly overrun the country. Only then does Goshtāsp recognize his error, and wishing both to make amends and save his rule, he sends his counselor, Jāmāsp, to release Esfandiyār and to promise him the throne if he will drive Arjāsp and his army out of Iran. Jāmāsp, however, does not mention the shah's offer but attempts to win Esfandiyār's support by speaking of the devastation his sisters and brothers have suffered at the hands of their enemies. At first Esfandiyār is unmoved by his pleas—none of his brothers and sisters have shown concern for his own suffering. When he learns that the one brother whom he loves, Farshidvard, has been brutally slain, the news stirs him to action at last. He shatters his bonds, too impatient to wait for the blacksmiths to do so, and sets out to rid Iran of the invading forces.

When Esfandiyār has defeated Arjāsp's army, Goshtāsp himself formally promises to yield his place to him, if he will first rescue his sisters from captivity in the enemy's capital—a fortress encircled with a brass wall. He gives him a royal crown as proof of his good intention and also presents him to the army as his heir. These are the promises that Esfandiyār alludes to when he confronts his father in court. If Goshtāsp now fears his son's eagerness to replace him on the throne, he has only himself to blame.

As the present story opens, Esfandiyār has returned in triumph from his campaign against Turān, where he freed his sisters, beheaded Arjāsp, and captured both Arjāsp's family and his treasury. His expectation is that Goshtāsp will now honor his promise and abdicate in his favor, but his father says and does nothing. Esfandiyār's explosive first scene is fueled by legitimate frustration, but it leads him to make a fatal error. In the heat of his anger and resentment he vows that if his father will not now make him shah, he will overthrow him and seize the throne by force: "I swear by great Yazdān, / Who holds the heavens up, I'll crown myself / Despite my royal father's wish" (11–12). In the world of the *Shahnameh*, challenges to royal authority invariably lead to the challenger's death, even when, as is true here, the threat is more rhetorical than real. This one moment of hotheaded rebelliousness is enough to assure Esfandiyār's destruction. It seems both cruel and unfair that a lapse in obedience that is so brief, and so justified, should be his death warrant. But fate, as Ferdowsi reminds us on many occasions, is as capricious as it is implacable.

In the event, the actual danger to Goshtāsp's monarchy vanishes with the morning sun. It is late and Esfandiyār is drunk when he makes his threat. He apparently thinks better of his angry words the next day and does not confront his father immediately, but only after several days' delay. His manner when he does is not threatening but earnest and pleading. Goshtāsp, forewarned of his son's anger, is able to smoothly deflect his protests by acknowledging their truth and insisting that he still intends to honor his promise. However, he says, there is one final task that Esfandiyār must undertake before he can be crowned. He must journey to Zābol and there humble its ruler, the legendary hero Rostam, for having shown an insulting reluctance to honor Iran's new royal line by attending them at court. Where Esfandiyār's first two tasks were both urgent and honorable, as were his earlier efforts to disseminate the new faith of Zoroastrianism, this new commission is neither. For centuries Rostam has performed heroic services for the shahs of Iran. Whatever his offense, he deserves better than this brutal insult. Esfandiyār knows this, and he senses that his father's intention is to do him some injury, not Rostam. His suspicions are well founded. Earlier, Goshtāsp, hearing of his son's frustration, had cast his horoscope and learned that Esfandiyārwas fated to die by Rostam's hand in Zābol. Although he cannot remedy that fate, he chooses neither to warn his son nor to delay his fatal encounter with Rostam but sends him off to blindly provoke the great hero's anger.

Even though he does not know what fate awaits him in Zābolestān, Esfandiyār would rather retire from the court than accept this commission. Once the shah orders him to do so, however, he has no choice but to obey. Both loyalty and ambition have been offered as motives for his decision to obey his father, but Esfandiyār's motive runs deeper than either of these. As a pious Zoroastrian he believes that the commands of his father, the shah, have the force of divine decree. If he disobeys him, he will suffer eternal torments in the afterlife. Once Goshtāsp has spoken, Esfandiyār has no choice but to raise an army and depart.

The shah's insistence that Rostam submit to having his hands and feet shackled, and that he make the journey to the court on foot, like a slave, comes as a terrible shock to Rostam. He is baffled by this show of hostility from a court that he has served so long and so well. He is more than willing to come to the court to receive whatever chastisement is his due, but, as Goshtāsp has surely anticipated, he is too proud to make the journey to the court on foot and with fetters on his hands and feet. The humiliation of this would be unendurable to him personally, and it also would have terrible consequences both for his own family and for his kingdom. To yield to such a disgrace would negate all that Rostam has been and done throughout his long life.

> I'll look upon your face with joyful heart
> And gladly do whatever you command.
> But not these chains! Shackles are shame, defeat,
> An ugly stain upon my family's name.
> While I'm alive, no one will ever see
> Me bound with chains. My soul insists on this. (516–518)

Esfandiyār has willingly endured shackles, and worse, at the shah's hands, but Rostam will not do so. The old hero does not feel himself threatened by the fires of eternal torment should he disobey the shah, or if he does, the destruction of his good name seems a heavier punishment. He cannot bring himself to obey a command that is both unreasonable and unjust even if it does come from the shah. In doing so, he too becomes a threat to the state, and, by the logic of the *Shahnameh*, he must be punished as well.

Esfandiyār deeply admires Rostam and is sympathetic to his sense of being ill used by the court. He has himself already suffered a more painful humiliation at the hands of his father than he would now, in his father's name, inflict upon Rostam. He attempts to mitigate the harshness of his father's command, promising that once they are at the court he will intercede with the shah on Rostam's behalf; yet if Rostam will not yield, he knows that he has no choice. He must obey the shah's command to the letter. Should he allow Rostam to approach the court mounted and free, as Rostam suggests, and not led by "a rope about his arms... on foot and running," like a slave, then his action will be counted by his father as outright disobedience. Goshtāsp, in short, has phrased his commission so that it will create an irresolvable conflict between Rostam and Esfandiyār.

Rostam welcomes Esfandiyār to Zābol with great warmth and admiration, and seems eager to befriend him. Esfandiyār cannot respond in kind, although he feels drawn to the ancient warrior. He must hide the very real affection and admiration he feels for him in order to carry out his father's wishes. There is a poignant moment, one of several, that shows what feelings Esfandiyār has been obliged to hide behind the mask of royal agent. It takes place just after the first, unsatisfactory encounter of the two heroes on the bank of the Hirmand River which marks the border between Iran and Sistān. Rostam has returned alone to his court to await Esfandiyār's invitation to dine, and Esfandiyār ponders how to continue their debate. He decides not to invite Rostam to eat with him because sharing a meal would draw them closer, and he anticipates that ties of friendship with Rostam will ultimately cause him pain. He muses aloud to his brother, Pashutan, whose principal function is to be the recipient of such confidences.

> ...We thought this was an easy task,
> But it's proved hard indeed. I have no wish
> To visit Rostam in his home, nor has
> He any need to see me here. Should he
> Not choose to come, I will not send for him.
> If one of us should breathe his last while here,
> His death will sear the heart of him who's left.
> A closer friendship would increase that grief. (541–54 4)

His words may seem cool, even harsh at first, but Esfandiyār believes that he himself is invincible and assumes that the heart that will be wounded will be his own. It is the thought of his own grief at Rostam's death that he finds unbearable. Such glimpses behind the mask that Goshtāsp has obliged him to wear reveal him to be an essentially decent man who is constrained by his piety and loyalty to betray his own instincts.

The exchanges between them inevitably become increasingly acrimonious as each tries, and fails, to persuade the other to his view. For the reader, as for Esfandiyār, there is a painful irony in Rostam's pleading with him to be more reasonable. Esfandiyār would gladly accept Rostam's conditions, but as his father's agent he must reject them. Nor, out of loyalty, can he reveal what his true thoughts and feelings are. He also knows that Goshtāsp only wishes him ill, but he cannot say this either. Indeed, when Rostam accuses Goshtāsp of perfidy Esfandiyār must appear to turn a deaf ear to Rostam and even defend the shah.

Hear me!. . .
I will not disobey the shah's command,
Not for a crown or throne. I find in him
Whatever's good or evil in this world.
My hell and heaven are contained in him. (858–860)

When, at last, they meet in battle, Rostam, at first, comes
perilously close to defeat, but through the magical intervention
of Simorgh he triumphs over Esfandiyār, although "triumph" is
surely the wrong word here. Their combat ends in the death of
Esfandiyār, but the outcome is as tragic for the ancient hero as it
is for the young shah. Esfandiyār loses his life and fails in his
ambition to rule Iran. He must look to receive the reward of his
virtue in heaven, not on earth. Rostam gains a brief respite from
defeat and death but does so at the cost of enduring shame for
having slain a brave and virtuous prince. Moreover, he does not
see himself as in any sense the victor in a battle. His only role
has been to act as fate's instrument in slaying Esfandiyār with
the deadly arrow made of tamarisk wood.

I was the agent of the tamarisk; that's all.
I am what's dark and dismal in this tale. (1441)

Rostam's role in this drama is, of course, more complex than
this. He is obliged here to reprise the role he played in the death
of his own son, Sohrāb. There are differences, of course. Sohrāb
explicitly threatened to overthrow the shahs of both Iran and
Turān, while Esfandiyār's challenge to his father, as we have
seen, is only in his father's mind. Rostam was unaware that the
young challenger he faced was his son until too late, while he is
all too aware of Esfandiyār's identity and of the consequences

his death will have for him. But the central fact of Rostam's killing a young hero who challenges royal authority, and of making a terrible personal sacrifice in order to preserve a bad ruler, remains unchanged. He has been absent from the central events of the *Shahnameh* quite literally for centuries. Now he has been called back to perform this terrible and onerous task. It is as though this is the price he must pay for his unique strength and skill, for enjoying Fate's favor throughout his long life.

His death follows closely on that of the young hero he slays and, indeed, is precipitated by it. The final chapter of Esfandiyār's life brings Rostam's life to its end as well. Rostam's presence, and the many similarities between these two remarkable and virtuous heroes, who serve two such deplorable rulers, seems meant to remind us of the terrible consequences of linking human frailty to divine right.

The final resolution of the tale returns the court of Iran to a state of order and security. Bahrām-Ardashir replaces his father as the acknowledged heir to the throne. Rostam is forgiven for not having shown proper respect to the court and reestablished in his rule of Zābolestān. Yet one is left with the sense of the world turned upside down, of the good being punished while the evil are rewarded. Each of the two heroes has in his own time been the chief prop and support of Iran and its shahs, and neither has done anything to threaten the security of the state. Bahman is in no sense the man his father was, and Shah Goshtāsp is the least admirable of rulers, a moral leper who is the real villain of the story. He provokes his son's anger by lying to him and forces him to fight Rostam, knowing he will be killed. He is the first and only shah to murder his own child, and he is condemned for his actions by the nobles of his court and his own family. He also goads Rostam into a fatal show of rebellion. Like Kay Kāvus, the foolish and arrogant shah whom Rostam served, Goshtāsp is so terrible a ruler for his country that we cannot help but question God's wisdom in choosing him. Worse yet, he is not punished for his sins.

I believe that questioning God's wisdom in choosing and supporting Goshtāsp as shah is precisely what Ferdowsi wishes us to do. He is no revolutionary. He accepts monarchy as the system that God has chosen to order human society. But in this magnificent and painful tale he has chosen to reveal to us the dark and shadowy side of that system. A bad monarch can be the enemy of all that is most admirable, and peace and security have been won here at a price that may be too heavy for society to bear. There is a bitter irony in the words that conclude the story of Rostam and Esfandiyār:

> The story of Esfandiyār has reached
> Its end at last. Long may the *shahriyār* live!
> His heart forever freed of care, the times
> Obedient to his command. May he
> Rejoice upon his famous throne, a rope
> Around the necks of those who wish him ill. (1664–1666)

The Family of Goshtāsp, Shāhanshāh of Iran

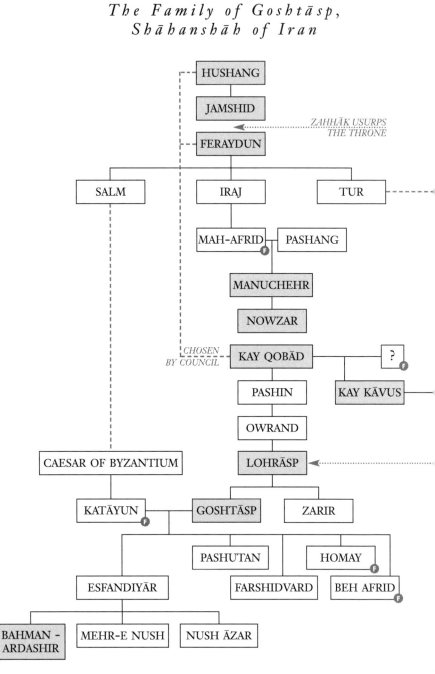

HUSHANG

JAMSHID

FERAYDUN — *ZAHHĀK USURPS THE THRONE*

SALM — IRAJ — TUR

MAH-AFRID — PASHANG

MANUCHEHR

NOWZAR

CHOSEN BY COUNCIL — KAY QOBĀD — ?

PASHIN — KAY KĀVUS

OWRAND

CAESAR OF BYZANTIUM — LOHRĀSP

KATĀYUN — GOSHTĀSP — ZARIR

PASHUTAN — HOMAY

ESFANDIYĀR — FARSHIDVARD — BEH AFRID

BAHMAN - ARDASHIR — MEHR-E NUSH — NUSH ĀZAR

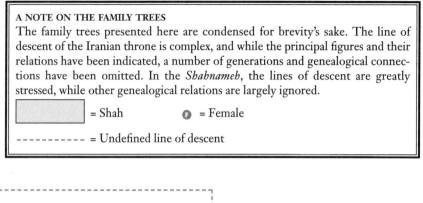

A NOTE ON THE FAMILY TREES
The family trees presented here are condensed for brevity's sake. The line of descent of the Iranian throne is complex, and while the principal figures and their relations have been indicated, a number of generations and genealogical connections have been omitted. In the *Shahnameh*, the lines of descent are greatly stressed, while other genealogical relations are largely ignored.

☐ = Shah   ⓕ = Female

‑ ‑ ‑ ‑ ‑ ‑ ‑ ‑ ‑ ‑ = Undefined line of descent

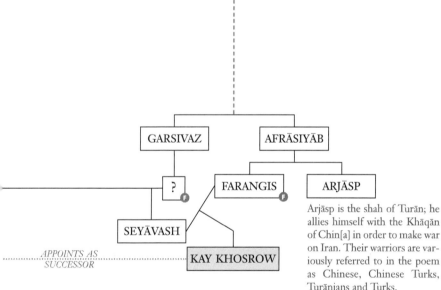

GARSIVAZ   AFRĀSIYĀB

?ⓕ   FARANGISⓕ   ARJĀSP

SEYĀVASH

APPOINTS AS SUCCESSOR   KAY KHOSROW

Arjāsp is the shah of Turān; he allies himself with the Khāqān of Chin[a] in order to make war on Iran. Their warriors are variously referred to in the poem as Chinese, Chinese Turks, Turānians and Turks.

The Family of Rostam, Ruler of Zābolestān

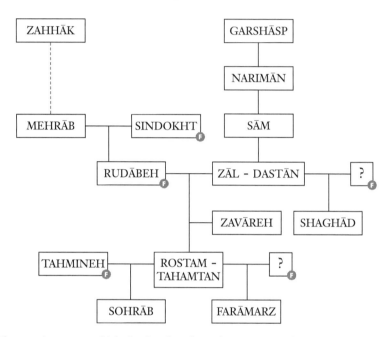

The province over which the family rules is known variously as Sistān, Zābol (the capital city), Zābolestān and Nimruz. They also rule over the city of Kābol and the region of Kābolestān, whose ruler is Mehrāb. At the end of the story Goshtāsp adds the province of Ghannuj, to Rostam's possessions.

PRONOUNCING PERSIAN NAMES

Persian names, whether of people or places, are stressed on the final syllable. This is true even when the name has three or more syllables. When a name has four syllables, there is a secondary stress on the second syllable so that the name is read as two iambs. Persian consonants are pronounced very much as they are in English with two exceptions. The grouping *kh* is pronounced as the *ch* in Bach. When *q* appears between vowels, it has a sound similar to the French *r*. At the beginning of a word the *q* sound is closer to *k*. Vowels should be pronounced as follows:

a	van, can		u	boot, loot
e	bet, set		ay	day, say
o	ode, rode		ow	low, toe
ā	calm, fall		āy	my, lie
i	tree, see			

Geography

BYZANTIUM (ROME): The Eastern Roman Empire that is Iran's neighbor to the west

GHANNUJ: An Indian city and province on the banks of the Ganges

GHAZNEYN: A major city in Khorasan

HĀMĀVARĀN: Roughly, present-day Yemen.

HIRMAND: A river that forms the present boundary between Iran and Afghanistan; in the *Shahnameh*, the border between Iran and Zābolestān

JAYHUN: A river in central Asia flowing from the Pamir Mountains to the Aral Sea. Once known as the Oxus, now called the Amu Darya

KĀBOLESTĀN/KĀBOL: A region, and capital city, in Central Asia and North India over which Rostam and his family rule

SĀRI: A city on the southern coast of the Caspian Sea.

SISTĀN: A large province in southeastern Iran to the east of the Hirmand in the *Shahnameh*, but to the west of it today. Also called Zābol, Zābolestān and Nimruz.

TURĀN: The kingdom (roughly, Central Asia) ruled over by Arjāsp, the son of Afrāsiyāb and enemy of Goshtāsp

ZĀBOLESTĀN/ZĀBOL: The name of the region over which Rostam and his ancestors rule, and that region's capital city

Section titles vary from manuscript to
manuscript and are not always used.
In this text, the titles are taken
from within the section.

The numbers in parentheses after each
title refer to the line numbers in:
Ja'far She'ār and Hasan Anvari
Razmnāmeh-ye Rostam va Esfandiyār
2nd edition (Tehran, 1373).

The Story of Rostam & Esfandiyār

Now is the time to drink delicious wine,
When fragrant scents float from the river's bank.
The earth is teeming and the heavens thunder.
Happy the man who cheers his heart with drink,
Who's rich in coins, and dainty foods, and well-
Filled cups; with sheep to slaughter for his guests.
I've none of these. Good luck to him who has.
May he be generous to those in need.
The garden's filled with roses; hyacinths
And tulips cover all the mountain slopes.
The nightingale laments throughout the glade
While the rosebud preens herself at his distress.
Since clouds are sending down their wind and rain,
I wonder why narcissus is so sad?
The nightingale wakes through the darkest night.
He laughs at wind and rain that set the rose
To trembling in fear. Snug in his perch
Within the rose, he sings his song. Meanwhile
The cloud roars like a lion, as though he were
The lover, not the rose. Winds tear his robe
To shreds. Fires flash within the thunderhead,
Fierce proofs of heaven's passion for the earth—

A love it offers here before the sun.
Who understands the nightingale's complaint?
Beneath the rose, what is it he laments?
Come, listen closely just at dawn, and hear
Him sing in Pahlavi* the tale of how
Esfandiyār was slain by brave Rostam,
Whose only memory of him is grief.
Like the roars of evening thunder, Rostam's cries
Will pierce the lion's ears and rend his heart.

HIS FATE AWAITS HIM IN ZĀBOLESTĀN (1–58)

I heard a story from the nightingale,
That he recited from some ancient songs.
One night Esfandiyār returned both drunk
And angry from his father's court. Although
The hour was late, he woke Queen Katāyun,
Great Caesar's child, who'd nurtured him both day
And night. When she drew near he called for wine,
And drinking deep, he told her his complaint:
"The shah, my father, has wronged me once again.
He promised me, 'If you will fearlessly
Revenge on Arjāsp Shah the slaying of
My father, Shah Lohrāsp, and free as well
Your sisters from their bonds, and if you'll weed
All evil from the garden of the world,†
Making it flourish once again, and so
Restore the honor of our name throughout
Iran, the army, throne and crown will all
Be yours, the royal treasury as well.'
Now when the heavens next lift up the sun,
And the shah, my father, wakes from sleep, I will

---

* Pahlavi is the literary dialect of Middle Persian.
† The weeding of the garden referred to here is a reference to Esfandiyār's campaign to defeat the army of Iran's principal enemy, Arjāsp, the shah of Turān and Chin—events narrated in earlier stories in this cycle.

Repeat the promises he's made to me—
Words he cannot deny. And if a frown
Should crease his brow, I swear by great Yazdān,
Who holds the heavens up, I'll crown myself
Despite my royal father's wish and give
The people of Iran their land. I'll crown
You queen of all and with a lion's strength
And heart make war upon our enemies."
His mother's heart was saddened by these words.
Her gown's fine silk seemed harsh as thorns. She knew
That Shah Goshtāsp would never make his son
The gift of crown and throne. She said to him,
"My son, you have endured so much. And yet,
What worldly power is there that your heart
Still yearns to have? If wealth and rule, royal
Authority and martial sway, you have
Them all. Don't look for more. Your father wears
A crown upon his head. The army and
The land belong to you. You know that when
He's gone, his crown and throne will both be yours,
As will his greatness, sovereignty and wealth.
What's better than a lionhearted son
Who loyally supports his father's rule?"
Esfandiyār replied with heat, "How wise
The man who said, 'Don't tell your secrets to
A woman, or else you'll hear them in the streets.
Do nothing that a woman may propose.
You won't meet one who has a grain of sense.'"
His words filled Katāyun with shame and fear.
He was abashed by what he'd said, as well.
Two days and nights Esfandiyār did not

Attend his father's court. He called for minstrels
To while the time away. He drank raw wine
And soothed his heart on a moon-faced maiden's breast.
But when three days had passed, Goshtāsp was told
His son was eager for his place. They said
His heart was filled with thoughts of throne and crown,
And that he longed for them both day and night.
The shah sent for his counselor, Jāmāsp
The wise, and for the seers who'd served Lohrāsp.
When they arrived, with books and charts in hand,
He asked, "What do the stars foretell for brave
Esfandiyār? Will he enjoy a life
That's long and calm, and filled with glory, too?
Is he to wear the emperor's crown? How long
Will sovereignty and fortune stand by him?"
Jāmāsp, the man of wisdom, heard the questions
His monarch asked and searched those ancient books.
What he saw there put wrinkles in his brow.
Grief filled his heart. He wept and said,[*] "Evil
The star that saw my birth! Evil the day
That I was born! Fire rained upon my head.
I wish that in the time of radiant Zarir
Some lion had devoured me or that
I'd not been born. Better I had not been
Alive that ill-starred day, so that I had
Not seen Zarir thrown to the earth like that,
His feet and legs all spattered with his gore.
How like Esfandiyār he was, from fear
Of whose attack the lion bursts its heart.
He has no equal in a fight. With one
Swift blow he sliced a dragon's trunk in two.

---

[*] Jāmāsp speaks here in an aside.

He cleansed the earth of all our enemies,
And freed us from the fear of wicked men.
His grief is yet to be endured—more pain
And bitterness that we must taste at last."
Goshtāsp addressed the sage: "Wise Jāmāsp, speak!
Leave nothing out, but tell us all you see!
Be quick! I want your answer now! I see
My question's made you frown. I fear that should
He lead the army like Zarir, my life
Will take a harmful turn, and soon. Who holds
His fate within his hand? Who is it that
Will cause us all to grieve and mourn?" The sage
Jāmāsp replied to him, "Great shah! Don't hold
This day too cheaply. His fate awaits him in
Zābolestān. The hand it lies within
Is that of Dastān's son, Rostam."
The shah had one more question for Jāmāsp:
"This dreadful fate, will it afflict me, too?
If I, the shāhanshāh* of all Iran,
Should yield the crown and throne to him, and if
He never looks upon Zābolestān,
Or far Kābolestān, will he escape
This awful fate? Will some auspicious star
Become his guide?" The sage astrologer,
Jāmāsp, replied, "No one can safely pass
That fateful wheel. Who has by wisdom or
By manliness escaped the knife-sharp claws
Of that celestial dragon? What has to be
Will be. There is no doubt. The shrewdest man
Has not escaped his fate." The thought of this
Grieved Goshtāsp's heart, and anguish burdened him.

---

* King of kings, i.e., emperor

But evil wishes and the turns of fate
Combined to guide him down a crooked path.

WHAT PRETEXT CAN YOU OFFER NOW? (59–100)

When night had gathered up its reins and fled,
And when the sun had raised his lance point high,
The shah ascended to his golden throne,
And radiant Esfandiyār approached.
He stood before him like a willing slave—
Distressed and anxious, hands upon his chest.
Then all the army gathered in the court,
The famous lords and heroes, too, with wise
Mobads* all facing him in line. Behind
Them stood the royal guard drawn up in ranks—
Esfandiyār, that fearsome elephant,
Brought forth his words with pain and hailed the shah.
"Long life to you, O radiant shah!" He said,
"Alone on earth yours is the light of God!†
By you are love and justice both made known.
By you are royal crown and throne adorned.
You are my father and my shah. I am
Your son and slave. You guide my every step.
When Arjāsp led his mounted Chinese troops
Into Iran, and sought to crush our faith,
I swore most solemn oaths before Izad‡
And took His sacred precepts as my guide.
Whatever man insults our faith, whose mind's
So twisted that he chooses images
To worship, not Izad, my sword will split
Him head to waist. I fear no man on earth.
So when Arjāsp, that leopard of the plain,

---

* Zoroastrian priests
† The word translated here is *farr*, a radiance or splendor that, in the
Shāhnāmeh, is often associated with the ruler of Iran.
‡ God

Attacked Iran, I did not flee the field.
Once, at a feast when you had called for food,
Gorazm's[*] hints made you dishonor me.
You bound my limbs with massive bolts and chains
That blacksmiths welded to great iron stakes.
You sent me to be held in Gombadān—
Brutal guards demeaned me there, while you
Abandoned Balkh[†] and fled to Zābol's court.
You would not face the blows of Arjāsp's sword,
Because you thought this war a kind of sport.
And so instead they fell on ancient Shah
Lohrāsp. When Jāmāsp came, he saw me bound,
My body wounded by those brutal chains.
He wished to see me on the throne instead,
And tried both long and hard to place me there.
I said to him, 'I'll leave these heavy chains
And hammered iron bolts just as they are
Since they were fixed here by the shah's command.
I do not want the army or the crown.
On Judgment Day I'll show these bonds to God
So He may judge the one who slandered me.'
He answered me, 'If you won't hear my plea,
You'll place a vicious man upon the throne.
So many noble chiefs,' he added then,
'Who bore their heavy maces into war,
Lie dead or wounded on the battlefield.
The hero Farshidvard lies with them there.
Your sisters have been captured by the Turks,[‡]
The shah, your father's fled, and writhes in shame
To think of you in chains. This terrible
And shameful news, does it not touch your heart?'

---

[*] An enemy of Esfandiyār
[†] Goshtāsp's capital city
[‡] Turānians

These things he said, and many more besides.
Such pain and grief accompanied his words!
I swiftly shattered all my bonds and shackles,
And hastened to the leader of my flock.
I slew more Turkish troops than one can count.
The shah was happy then with all my deeds.
Should I recount my seven labors one
By one, my words would never reach their end.
I glorified the name of Shah Goshtāsp,
Severed the head of Shah Arjāsp, and brought
His wife and children with me to this court,
His crown and throne and treasury as well.
You've had the joy of spending Arjāsp's wealth.
Blood, sweat and pain have been my share.
Despite the broken promises, despite
The chains, I have not slighted your command.
You've said repeatedly, 'Should I look on
Your face once more, I'll choose you willingly
To be my heir, and I'll entrust my crown
And ivory throne to you. By manliness
And bravery you've earned the right to rule.'
Before these great and noble lords, such words
Disgrace me now. They ask, 'Where is your army;
And where your treasury?' What pretext can
You offer now? Why am I here? For what
Have I endured this labor and this pain?"

THERE'S NOT A MAN TO EQUAL YOU— EXCEPT ROSTAM (101–150)

The shah, Goshtāsp, responded to his son,
"To turn aside from truth would not be right.

You've done far more than you report. May He
Who made the earth be ever at your side.
In all the world I see no public and
No private foe of ours who hears your name
And does not writhe in dread. No, more than that,
Who hears your name and does not die of fear.
There's not a man to equal you—except
Rostam, Dastān's unwise but famous son.
To him belong for life the lands of Bost,
Kābol, Ghazneyn and all Zābolestān.
His bravery's so great it's made him proud.
He holds himself subordinate to none.
He was a servant at the court of Kay
Kāvus,* and that of Kay Khosrow as well,
But will not stoop to mention Shah Goshtāsp.
'His crown is new,' he says, 'while ours is old.
No hero in the world can equal me,
Not in Turān or Rome, nor in Iran.'
Go now, at once! Ride to Sistān, and there
Make use of all your strength, deceit and guile.
Draw forth your sword and mace. Bind brave Rostam,
The son of Zāl, in chains and bring him here.
His brother, Zavāreh, and Farāmarz,
His son, as well. Nor let them ride one pace.
When you've performed the task I set you now
You'll hear no further caviling from me.
But by the Heavenly Judge who gives us strength,
Who lights the sun and moon and all the stars,
I'll yield the crown to you and seat you on
The throne as sovereign of the royal court."
Esfandiyār replied, "O noble shāh,

---

* An energetic and foolish shah who was rescued from many misadventures
by Rostam's heroism

You stray too far from ancient custom here.
You would be wise to speak more moderately.
Make war instead upon the Chinese shah,
Defeat in battle all that famous court.
But why attack a single, aged man,
Whom Kay Kāvus once called the lion's scourge?
From Manuchehr* to Kay Qobād, the heart
Of every shah has been rejoiced by him.
In all Iran there's been no finer man,
And none who's done so many worthy deeds.
They named him Lord of Rakhsh,† Lion Slayer,
World Conqueror, and Giver of the Crown.
His fame is great and not some recent thing.
His lands were given him by Kay Khosrow.
If royal grants like these are worthless now,
Why should he seek another from Goshtāsp?"
The shah responded to Esfandiyār,
"O virtuous and lion-hearted prince,
The acts of one who turns his back on God
Are nullified and scattered to the wind.
You've heard of how Eblis‡ once led Kāvus
Astray. He tried to fly up to the heavens
On eagles' wings but fell, lamenting, to
The waters off Sāri instead. In far
Hāmāvarān he wed a demon's child
And made her queen of all his wives. It was
Her enmity that slew brave Seyāvash
And brought confusion to the royal house.
One should not cross the threshold of a man
Who violates his trust with God. If you
Would have a crown and throne from me, then raise

---

* A just shah in whose reign Rostam was born
† Rakhsh was Rostam's legendary steed and companion in his adventures.
‡ The devil

An army now, at once, and lead it to
Zābolestān. Once there, bind Rostam's hands,
And lead him here, a rope about his arms.
Do not allow Dastān or Farāmarz
Or Zavāreh to set their traps for you.
Bring him on foot and running to this court.
Drag him before the troops for all to see.
No man will scorn my rule from that day on,
However great or wealthy he may be."
The army's leader spoke as anger creased
His brow. "O shah of all the world," he said,
"Turn back from this. Your purpose here is not
Rostam or Zāl. You seek Esfandiyār.
You would not yield your place to any man,
And so you'd have me vanish from the earth.
Let the crown and throne of all the Kays* be yours,
And mine a single corner of this world.
I'll be your loyal servant there as well
And humbly bow my head to your command."
Goshtāsp replied, "Don't speak so angrily.
This greatness will be yours, do not despair.
Come, from the army here, choose all the men
That you will need—battle-tried veterans
Prepared for war. Troops, provisions, weapons—
Take all you need. Then let your foe despair.
Without you what are throne or wealth to me?
Of what use then are soldiers or a crown?"
Esfandiyār replied, "For me, as well,
An army will not be of any use.
If death has come for me, the Keeper of
The World won't hold it back for all this host."

He left the court both angry and confused.
He'd lost a throne and gained his father's wrath.
With heavy heart, and sighs upon his lips,
Esfandiyār returned to his own court.

DON'T FACE THAT RAGING ELEPHANT ALONE! (151–187)

Distressed and fearful when she heard, his mother,
Queen Katāyun, rushed weeping to her son,
The fortunate Esfandiyār. "O prince,
Who calls to mind all shahs who've ruled the earth,
Bahman has told me that you'll shortly leave
This palace for Kābol, and that, once there,
You plan to bind the lord of mace and sword,
Rostam, the son of Zāl, with heavy chains.
By all the world, hear my advice my son.
Don't hasten to this hateful task, not now!
This warrior is an elephant in strength
And sets Niles of blood to flowing on the earth.
He tore the White Div's* heart right from his chest
And drives the sun from its own path. He slew
Hāmāvarān's bright moon, Queen Sudābeh.
Yet none dared challenge him, not with a word.
Surely, there was no horseman who could equal
The brave Sohrāb upon the field of war.
Yet when he battled with his father, hand
To hand, recall how quickly he was slain.
Afrāsiyāb slew Seyāvash, and in
Revenge, Rostam plunged all the world in blood.
A curse upon this throne and crown, and on
This devastation and this waste of life!
Don't lose your head to gain a crown, my son.

---

* A *div* is a demon; some divs, such as the White Div, are named.

No shah's been born with one upon his head.
Your father has grown old, but you are young.
In strength and courage you're the better man.
The army's hopes are fixed on you as well.
Don't risk disaster out of rage. Sistān
Is not the only place where you may go.
Be wise as well as brave. Do nothing rash.
Please, heed your mother's words! Don't make me mourn
For you both now and in the world to come!"
Esfandiyār replied, "Dear loving mother,
Please hear me now. The *pahlavān*,* Rostam,
Is just the man you say he is; it's true.
You chant his virtues like the sacred *Zand*.†
However long and hard you try, you will
Not find a better man in all Iran,
And since it can't be right to bind him so,
The shah's command will end in bad, not good.
And yet you should not so dishearten me.
For if you do, I will despair and die.
How can I disobey the shah? How can
I turn my back upon a court like this?
If fate awaits me in Zābolestān,
My star will surely draw me there. And should
Rostam submit to my command, he will
Not hear a harsh or unkind word from me."
The lashes of his mother's eyes rained blood.
She tore her hair and cried. "You are too strong,"
She said. "And so you hold your soul too lightly.
Your strength is that of some fierce elephant,
And yet it will not be enough. Don't leave
Here unattended by a host of men.

---

* Noble hero or knight
† The commentary on the sacred Zoroastrian book, the *Avesta*. In English,
the two works are united in a single name, *Zendavesta*.

Don't take your life into your hands like this
Don't face that raging elephant alone.
If you decide to risk your life this way,
It's evil Ahriman* whose ends are served.
Don't lead your sons into this hell, or else
No man of sense will think your mind is clear."
Her warrior son replied, "It would not be
Advisable to leave them here. When young
Men stay behind and wait, as women do,
Their temperaments turn foul and dark. I say
A youth must go to every war and in
Whatever place. Each blow he strikes is with
His monarch's mace. I have no need for troops,
Except some horsemen and my household guards."
Queen Katāyun departed from her son,
Deep pain and dark foreboding filled her soul.
For love of him she wept the night away.

WHEN HE CONFRONTS HIS FATE
A MAN SHOULD SMILE (188–216)

Next morning, as the cocks began to crow,
The sound of drums arose within the court.
Like some fierce elephant Esfandiyār
Mounted his horse; then swift as smoke, he led
His warriors on their way. They marched in order
Until the road divided. There they paused. One way
Would lead them to the fortress Gombadān,†
The other turned a little toward Sistān.
A camel, the one before Esfandiyār,
Sank to the earth. Although its driver beat
It savagely, it lay there like a stone.

---

* The God of Darkness, the evil twin of Ahura Mazda (the God of Light)
† This is the fortress in which Esfandiyār was imprisoned by his father.

The caravan could not advance one step.
This seemed an evil omen to the shah.
He ordered them to hack the beast in two
So that this baleful sign would stay with it
And leave him only God's bright radiance.
The soldiers there cut off its head, and so
Its evil star declined. The camel vexed
Esfandiyār at first, but he dismissed
This heavy portent from his mind. "A man
Who's been victorious in life," he said,
"Will shed his fortune's light upon the world.
Since good and bad are both the gifts of God,
When he confronts his fate, a man should smile."
From there, still fearful of calamity,
They marched toward the Hirmand River's bank,
Then made their camp according to their plan,
Set up the palace tents and placed a throne
Beneath a canopy where fortunate
Esfandiyār might sit. He called for wine
And minstrels, filling their hands with gold and gems.
With wine and music he rejoiced his heart,
The hearts of all his noble lords as well.
The ancient vintage turned the faces of
The warrior shah* and all his men rose red.
He told his comrades, "I have not shirked the shah's
Command, and yet I've gone astray." He said,
"Go, arm yourself to fight with Dastān's son!
Don't hesitate to burden him with chains
And with disgrace. I've come to carry out
My father's wish. This ancient pahlavān
Has served our rulers well. His heavy mace

---

* The term "shah" is also used for princes of royal blood such as
Esfandiyār and for lesser monarchs such as Rostam.

43

Subdued the world for them. All of Iran,
From proudest monarch to the humblest slave
Endures through Rostam's strength. But now
A valiant envoy must be sent to him,
Some wise and clever man, well-spoken, too—
A noble horseman robed in grandeur and
Good sense, who won't be caught by Rostam's tricks.
If he'll submit to us, he'll lighten all
Our dark and gloomy thoughts. If he'll accept
These manacles from me of his own will,
By this wise act he'll bind the hand of mischief.
I wish him only what is good, so long
As he will keep rebellion from his thoughts."
"This is the way," wise Pashutan replied.
"Hold firm to it, and honor noble worth."

YOU'VE LAID ASIDE THE ROBES OF SERVITUDE (217–282)

He ordered that his son, Bahman, approach
And counseled him at length. "Take my black horse,"
He said, "But first array yourself in robes
Of Chinese silk, and wear a crown that's set
With kingly gems. Whoever sees you then,
Although you are surrounded by a host
Of warriors, will recognize your birth
And cry aloud in wonder to Yazdān.
Take five remounts as well, caparisoned
In gold, and ten distinguished mobads, too.
Proceed directly to the palace of
Rostam, but do not force the pace. Greet him
From us, and show him every courtesy.
Speak graciously and well to him, and say,

'The man who in this life attains great heights,
Who rules vast lands yet stays unharmed by ill,
Must thank our Generous Lord repeatedly.
Whoever knows the good and honors it,
If he grows strong in virtue and abstains
From all that's wrong, his fortune will increase
As he lives happy in this fleeting world.
And if he holds himself apart from all
Unworthy actions now as well, he will
Obtain by this the paradise to come.
The man possessed of wisdom knows that good
And bad will both pass quickly by. Our bed
At last will be dark earth. Our souls will fly
To our Pure Lord. Whoever in this world
Has known the good has humbly served his shah.
The crop you plant is what you harvest, too.
The words you speak are those you'll hear in turn.
Let's take your measure justly now and strive
Not to exceed the mark, nor yet fall short.
You're one who's lived through countless years, and in
That time how many shāhanshāhs you've seen!
Yet you yourself, if you will wisely judge,
Must recognize that this is undeserved.
You have such wealth and greatness, such troops
And precious horses, a throne and crown as well.
It was my forebears who conferred these gifts
On you because you'd always served them well.
The realm of Shah Lohrāsp filled half the world.
And yet you never journeyed to his court.
When he conferred the throne of Persia on
His son, Goshtāsp, you neither came to serve

Him there nor sent a letter in your place.
You've laid aside the robes of servitude
And wish there were no monarchs left on earth.
From Hushang, Jamshid and Feraydun,* who slew
Zahhāk† and seized his throne, down to the time
Of Kay Qobād, of all who've worn the crown
Of Feraydun, who is there equal to
Goshtāsp? In fighting, feasting, wise counsel and
The hunt, he stands above them all. When he
Received the pure and noble faith,‡ error
And unbelief both disappeared. The way
Before the shah is radiant as the sun,
False teaching and the faith the divs pursue
Are lost in night. And after that Arjāsp
First threatened war, his troops all leopards and
Their captains crocodiles. The noble shah
Rode out to meet that vast and fearful horde,
And made a graveyard of the battlefield.
The earth's broad face could not be seen. Those great
In war will tell this tale 'til Judgment Day.
From east to west the world belongs to him.
His blows have broken every lion's back.
The land that stretches from Turān up to
The gates of India and Rome is his.
The world is pliant wax within his hands.
The desert tribes attend his court as well
And send him yearly tribute since they are,
In short, too weak to challenge him in war
I've told you all of this, brave pahlavān,
Because the shah is vexed at heart with you.
You have not come to serve him at his court,

---

* Legendary shahs of Iran
† The foreign, tyrant shah who gained his throne with the devil's aid
‡ Zoroastrianism. Zoroaster appeared during the reign of Goshtāsp, who
not only converted to the new faith but vigorously promoted it among

46

Nor shown his nobles due esteem. You have
Withdrawn instead and hide yourself from view.
Yet how, unless they purge their minds and hearts
Of everything, can those at court forget
Rostam? You've sought the good in every way,
Obeying each and every shah in turn.
If one should reckon up your labors' worth,
It far exceeds your wealth. Sadly, none of
The shahs you've served would see this as I do.
Goshtāsp has said to me, "Rostam has such
Great wealth in lands and stored up treasure,
That now he sits and drinks the time away.
What profit is a drunk to any man?"
One day he grew enraged and swore an oath,
That by bright day and cobalt night, he would
Not see you in his court—except in chains.
And so I've hastened to Zābolestān.
The shah's command was that I not delay.
Be careful now, avoid his royal wrath.
Have you not seen him when rage filled his eyes?
When you have come to court as he commands,
And made your soul the pledge of your reform,
Then by the shining sun and Zarir's soul,
And by my lion father's life as well,
I'll make Goshtāsp repent of what he's done.
The stars and moon will shine on you once more.
I seek no profit for myself in this.
I neither lie nor cheat in any task.
My only guides are wisdom and the truth,
This Pashutan, my brother, will affirm.
I've calmed my father's anger for your sake,

---

his own and neighboring kingdoms. It was Esfandiyār who actively car-
ried on this campaign.

Although I thought you guilty of the charge.
But he's the shah; I'm his subordinate.
I'll never disobey the shah's decree.
Now you must sit and counsel with your kin—
With Zāl, your father, and with Zavāreh,
With Farāmarz as well, and with the wise
And famous Rudābeh. Weigh all my words
Out one by one. You'll see that I am right.
The heroes of my father's army wish
To devastate your land. That must not be.
When I have brought you to the court in chains,
I'll castigate my father for this crime.
We'll stand before his throne and plead your case,
And so transform his wrath to calm and peace.
Upon the honor of my family's name
I won't allow harsh winds to blow on you.'"

A WARLIKE KNIGHT HAS REACHED THIS SHORE (283–314)

Once he had heard the shah's, his father's, words,
Bahman prepared himself to leave the camp.
He dressed himself in royal gold brocade
And set a princely crown upon his head.
He rode forth proudly from the palace tent,
His shining standard fluttering behind.
Then with his head held high, and mounted on
A noble horse, he crossed the Hirmand's stream.
A watchman spied him as he neared the bank
And cried aloud toward Zābolestān,
"A warlike knight has reached this shore. He rides
A jet-black horse with ornaments of gold!
He's followed by a troop of horsemen, too."

At once the golden Zāl, with mace in hand
And lasso at his saddle bow, mounted
His horse and rode where he might see this youth.
He studied him, then sighed aloud and said,
"I'm sure this is some famous pahlavān.
Those royal robes show he's of noble birth.
He must be of Shah Lohrāsp's line. God grant
His coming to this land proves fortunate!"
He left the sentry and rode back to court—
So lost in thought it seemed he was asleep.
Bahman appeared before the palace gate,
His royal banner flying by his side.
Not knowing Zāl, he shrugged his royal shoulders
And called aloud to him, "Noble countryman!
Where is the son of Zāl, this people's chief,
The staff that holds the age erect? The hero,
Esfandiyār, has journeyed to Zābol
And pitched his tents upon the Hirmand's bank."
Zāl answered him: "My dear, impetuous youth,
Dismount, take up a cup of wine and rest!
Rostam is hunting now with Zavāreh
And Farāmarz, but he'll return quite soon.
You and your men may wait for him within.
Dismount and rest! Rejoice your hearts with wine!"
Bahman replied, "Esfandiyār did not
Command that I should pause to drink or pass
The time with song. Appoint a man who knows
The mountain roads to guide me on the way.
I'll go where Rostam hunts." "What is your name?"
Zāl asked, "Why have you come, and why such haste?
You must be of Shah Lohrāsp's family

49

Or else a son of Shah Goshtāsp himself."
"I am Bahman," he said, "the son of him
Who has no peer, whose body's made of brass."*
When he had heard the noble youth's reply,
The golden Zāl dismounted and bowed low.
Bahman alighted then as well and smiled.
The two exchanged some further words as well.
Once more the ancient Zāl insisted that
He linger there awhile. "This haste does not
Seem right," he said. But Prince Bahman was firm.
"One must not slight Esfandiyār's commands."
Zāl chose a man, Shir Khun, a seasoned guide,
Who knew the way quite well, and sent them off.
He led them on their way for many miles.
At last he pointed out the hunting ground,
Then turned his horse and galloped back to court.

I HAVE A MESSAGE FROM ESFANDIYĀR (315–370)

A mountain rose before the youthful prince.
He spurred his horse ahead and looked toward
The hunting ground below. From there he saw
The figure of the pahlavān Rostam,
Who grasped a tree trunk in one hand. A crowd
Of guides and huntsmen sat around the fire.
His mace and hunting gear were placed close by.
A stallion onager† was spitted on that tree,
While in his other hand he held a cup
Of ruby wine. Bold Farāmarz, his son,
Was standing in attendance at his side.
Rakhsh grazed at will. There was a meadow there,
With trees and grass, through which a river flowed.

---

* The epithet "brass-bodied" is given to Esfandiyār because his body was
impervious to any weapon.
† A wild ass (*Equus hemionus*) native to central Asia and famous for being
both fleet and tasty

"Is this Rostam," he thought, "or has the sun
Just risen in the west? In all the world,
No one has seen his equal, nor ever heard
Of one among the heroes of past times.
If they should meet upon the battlefield,
I fear that brave Esfandiyār will be
No match for him and will be forced to flee.
Let me destroy him now with some great stone
And break the hearts of Zāl and Rudābeh."
He pried a boulder from the granite peak
And sent it hurtling down the mountainside.
Rostam's brother, Zavāreh, first spied
The rock and heard its rumbling from below.
"Rostam! Look out! A boulder's rushing down
The slope toward you!" To Zavāreh's distress,
Rostam refused to stir a foot, or lay the spit
Aside, but waited as the avalanche
Came closer still, its dark dust shadowing
The mountain's slope, then raised his boot, and with
A single kick, he sent it from his path.
His brother and his son both cheered Rostam's
Exploit. But Bahman was dismayed to see
The strength and skill of this, his father's foe.
"If radiant Esfandiyār should meet
An enemy like this upon the field,
He will be humbled in the fight or slain.
One must use caution in confronting him.
Should Tahamtan defeat Esfandiyār,
He'll seize the kingdom of Iran as well."
Then, seated on his swift-paced horse, and lost
In thought, he rode down from the mountain peak.

He told the mobads of the miracle
He'd seen, rejecting now the easy path.
As they drew closer to the hunting ground,
Rostam observed them on the road and asked
A mobad standing near, "Who is that man? I think
He must be kin to Shah Goshtāsp." Then he
Rode out with Zavāreh and all those at
The camp to meet them on the road. As swift
As smoke Bahman dismounted from his horse
To greet Rostam with compliments. "Until I learn
Your name," Rostam replied, "you won't get what
You wish from me." "I am Bahman," he said,
"The famous son of brave Esfandiyār, and chief
Among the lords who honor truth."
Tahamtan hugged him firmly to his chest,
Apologizing for his tardiness.
They went, the two of them, toward the camp
Together with their loyal retinues.
When he was seated there he gave Rostam
The greetings of Goshtāsp and all his court.
Bahman then said, "The prince, Esfandiyār,
Has ridden from the court as swift as fire
And pitched his camp upon the Hirmand's bank.
This he has done at Shah Goshtāsp's command.
If the knightly pahlavān will hear it now,
I have a message from Esfandiyār."
Rostam replied, "The Shah's command to me,
I hold as higher than the moon and sun.
But first let's eat the food that we have here,
Then we and all the world are yours to rule."
He spread a cloth on which he placed fresh bread,

An onager as well, hot from the fire.
And while he placed the cloth before Bahman,
He spoke to him of former times. Alone
Of all the courtiers gathered there, he called
His brother, Zavāreh, to sit by him.
He placed a second buck before himself—
He ate an onager at every meal.
He salted it and cut it up and ate,
While Bahman watched his every move with care.
He ate a portion of his meat as well,
But not one-tenth of what Rostam devoured.
Tahamtan smiled at him and said in jest,
"Shahs have their courts to feast abundantly.
When you enjoy your food no more than this,
Why did you undertake the seven labors?
And if you eat no more than this, my lord,
How can you wield a spear upon the field?"
"We men of royal birth," Bahman replied,
"Are pledged to neither eat nor talk too much.
Who eats but little fights the more, we say,
And risks his life more readily in war."
Rostam laughed long at this and shouted out,
"Such manliness should not be hid from us!"
He filled a golden cup with wine and with
It drank a toast to free and noble men.
He placed another cup in Bahman's hand:
"Take this and drink the health of whom you wish!"
But Bahman paused, afraid to drink the wine.
So Zavāreh first took a draught and said,
"O prince of Goshtāsp's line, I pray that you'll
Take pleasure in the drinking of this wine!"

53

Once more he grasped the wine cup in his hand,
And took a sip, but with an anxious heart.
His mind was filled with wonder at Rostam—
His neck and chest and fearful appetite.
They mounted then and rode, Bahman beside
The famous knight. He gave him greetings from
The brave and worthy knight, Esfandiyār,
And spoke his message to him word by word.

DON'T LOOK UPON THE WORLD
LIKE SOME RAW YOUTH (371–425)

The ancient warrior was troubled by
Prince Bahman's words. "I've heard the message that
You bring," he said, "and I am greatly pleased
To see you here. Take this reply from me
To brave Esfandiyār: 'Pre-eminent
And gallant lord! A man who's wise, and looks
Into the heart of things, should he possess
Great wealth and manliness, be blessed with triumphs
And celebrated for his noble name
Among the great and famous of this world,
A man like this,—as you, my lord, now are—
Should not be evil-minded and unfair.
Let us be just in this, like godly men,
Not clasp the hand of wrong within our own.
Some words are better left unsaid. They're like
A tree that has no scent and gives no fruit.
If your heart chooses avarice, that path
Will lead you on for many years. A shah
Should speak in measured words, or none. It's better
To be silent than speak ill. You would have pleased

Your servant if you'd said, "No mother's borne
A noble son like you. You far exceed
The mark your forebears set in manliness
And martial skill, in speech and counsel, too.
Your fame has reached Byzantium, China,
India and the Land of Sorcerers[*] as well."
I would have thanked you for such words and praised
Your name three watches of the day and night.
I've long implored Yazdān to bring you here
That I might have the joy of seeing you—
Your handsome face, your warrior's bravery
And strength, your royal kindliness as well.
I'd hoped that we might sit together in
Good cheer and toast the health of Shah Goshtāsp.
Now all I sought I've found. I've hastened here
To ask that you accept my invitation.
I've come alone, with neither troops nor guards,
To hear from you the shah's command. I'll bring
You all the grants just shahs have given me,
From Kay Khosrow on back to Kay Qobād.
And now, great shah, consider well what I
Have done and what endured. If the reward
For all my labor, the pain I've suffered and
The loyalty of many, many years
Is to be wounded by the Shah and wear
Such shackles on my feet, it would be best
To never see the earth. Or, seeing it,
To not remain here long. I'll come to you
And boldly tell my secrets to the world.
Then bind my arms with rope, and hang me by
My feet with thongs of leopard hide, as I

---

[*] It is not known what region is being referred to here as "the Land of
Sorcerors" (*jādustān*).

Once bound a raging elephant's neck and threw
Him in the Nile. If now some sin of mine
Is brought to light, cut off my head. But spare
Me these insulting words. Torture the hearts
Of demons with abuse like this, but do
Not say to me what none has said before.
Don't cage the wind and call it manliness.
Great men don't pass through fire by choice, or plunge
Into the sea, not knowing how to swim.
The shining of the sun cannot be hidden,
Nor can one mate a lion with a fox.
Don't cast a challenge in my path. I am,
Myself, the stuff that challenges are made of.
No one's placed fetters on my legs, and no
Fierce elephant has forced me from my place.
Act now as princes should, and turn aside
From what would be unworthy. Empty your heart
Of anger and of vengeance as one should.
Don't look upon the world like some raw youth.
Be cheerful, and cross the river to this side.
The pure Yazdān will give you welcome. Come.
Make our home precious by your presence here.
Do not withhold yourself from me. As I
Once served Qobād, I'll serve you now. When you
Have come, you and your troops, you may delight
Yourselves a full two months. Both men and beasts
Will be refreshed, while those who'd do you harm
Go blind with envy. Game covers the plains,
Wildfowl the rivers and lakes. And even if
You stay much longer, you won't grow restless.
Let me behold in you the warrior's strength

As you slay lions and tigers with your sword.
When you would lead your army to Iran,
And to the court of Shah Goshtāsp, their chief,
I'll open up my ancient treasuries,
Those that I've gathered by my sword, and place
Before you all that I've acquired by strength
Of arms through many years. Take what you wish,
And give the rest away as gifts. But don't
Dismay my heart on such a day as this.
Reward your troops, and generously. When you
Are met with good, do not respond with harsh
Severity. When it is time for you
To leave, and to return to court, I'll ride
Beside you on the road and come into
The presence of Goshtāsp with head erect.
I'll soften his wrath by my apologies
And humbly kiss his head and eyes and feet.
I'll ask the wise and noble shah, "Why have
You ordered that my feet be bound with chains?'"
Remember now each word I've spoken here,
Report them all to great Esfandiyār."

WHAT ANSWER DID THE FAMOUS CHAMPION GIVE? (426–538)

Bahman heard his answer, then left the camp,
The godly mobad riding by his side.
Tahamtan paused a moment by the road.
He beckoned Zavāreh to him, his son,
Brave Farāmarz, as well. "Go to Dastān
And Kābol's moon, wise Rudābeh, at once.
Say that Esfandiyār has come to us,
And come with hopes of ruling all the world.

Set up a golden throne within the court.
Adorn it royally with cloths like those
We used in Shah Kāvus's time, but still
More rich and fine. Prepare a feast as well,
Sumptuous dishes befitting his high rank.
The royal heir has come to visit us
But filled with anger and keen to fight.
He is a famous hero and brave shah
Who would not hesitate to charge a field
Of lions. I'll go invite him now. If he
Accepts, we all may hope for good from this.
If he seems well disposed toward me, I'll give
The prince a crown all set with gold and rubies.
I won't begrudge him wealth or precious gems,
Nor mace and sword, nor armor for his horse.
But if bright fortune does not shine for us,
And he should disappoint my hopes, you know
That with my twisted rope I've caught and bound
The necks of many raging elephants."
Zavāreh replied, "There is no fear of that.
No one seeks battle when there is no cause.
For wisdom and for bravery, there's none
Who's like Esfandiyār in all the world.
A wise man won't engage in evil acts,
Nor have we injured him in any way."
Zavāreh rode back to Zāl. Rostam, perplexed,
Sighed once and shrugged his shoulders, then set out.
He galloped swiftly toward the Hirmand's bank,
Alert and fearful of the ill to come.
He reined his horse in as he neared the stream
And waited for Bahman to greet him there.

Meanwhile, Bahman entered the camp and went
At once to stand before his father's throne.
Esfandiyār the fortunate inquired,
"What answer did the famous champion give?"
On hearing this, he sat before his father,
And point by point, he told him all he'd heard.
He gave him greetings from Rostam at first
And then recited his reply. He told
His father all that he had seen and what
He'd understood from it as well. "No one
Has seen his like in any company.
He has a lion's heart, the body of
An elephant enraged. He's strong enough
To drag a crocodile out of the Nile.
He's come to Hirmand's bank, unarmed—without
His helmet or his greaves, with neither rope
Nor mace. He has some need to meet with you,
But why he does is still unknown to me."
Esfandiyār flared up at this and shamed
Bahman before the courtiers. "It is
Not fitting when we tell our secrets to
Our wives. And if one sends a boy on some
Great task, he won't be brave or confident.
When have you heard the coughing of a fox?
What have you seen of men and war? But now
You've made Rostam a fierce and warlike
Elephant to frighten this brave gathering."
But privately he said to Pashutan,
"This warlike lion's still a youth it seems.
His body is still sound despite his years."
He ordered them, "Go, saddle my black horse!

Cinch tight my golden saddle on his back!"
One hundred of the army's finest horsemen
Rode with Esfandiyār the fortunate.
Galloping they reached the Hirmand's stream,
Their lassoes coiled and ready on their saddles.
Rakhsh whinnied loudly from this side. From that
The *shahriyār*'s* horse replied, both hastening
To meet. When they had neared the river's side
Tahamtan left the bank and plunged into
The water. He dismounted there and greeted
Esfandiyār: "Long have I prayed to God,
The One, that he would be your guide and bring
You here both safe and sound, your army and
The famous nobles of your court as well.
Let's sit somewhere and speak together now.
We'll ask and answer questions each in turn,
And share our best and most auspicious thoughts.
I swear, with God as witness to my words,
That wisdom is my only guide. I do
Not seek advantage for myself in this,
Nor do I lie in anything I do.
Were I to see the face of Seyāvash
Before me now, I would rejoice no less.
Indeed, there's no one you resemble more
Than generous and kingly Seyāvash.
Fortunate the shah who has a son like you!
Whose height and majesty fill him with pride.
Fortunate the people of Iran who bow
Before your throne and your unsleeping fortune.
Wretched the one who'd challenge you.
He'll know defeat, head cast into the dust.

---

* Another term for shah

May all your enemies be filled with fear,
The hearts of all your foes be split in two.
May your fortune ever be triumphant,
And each dark night become Noruz* for you."
Esfandiyār, when he had heard this welcome,
Dismounted from his famous horse and clasped
Great-bodied Rostam to his chest. And then,
Content, he praised his host in turn. "I thank
The Lord of All, great pahlavān, that I
Should see you here alert and full of joy.
It's right to speak your praise. The heroes of
The world are like the earth beneath your feet.
Fortunate the man who has a son like you.
He sees a branch that's laden with ripe fruit.
Fortunate the father who has a prop like you
For he's secure from fortune's cruelty.
And fortunate is Zāl, who, when his time
Is done, will leave behind a son like you!
I looked at you and thought of lionlike
Zarir, great hunter, warrior and chief."
"Oh wise and noble pahlavān," Rostam
Replied, "who holds the world within his hands,
And is alert of mind and wise of soul,
Grant me one wish, and I will be content.
Approach my home in state. To see you there
Will fill my soul with light. Although it is
Not worthy of a shah, we'll make the best
Of what there is and so content ourselves."
Esfandiyār replied to him and said,
"O emblem of the world's great pahlavāns!
A man who is pre-eminent like you,

---

* A festival held on the vernal equinox to herald the start of the new year

Who gladdens all who dwell within Iran,
To ignore your invitation, slight your home
Or disregard your place would not be right.
And yet, I can't ignore the shah's commands,
Not publicly nor privately. Goshtāsp
Instructed me to neither pause here in
Zābol nor war upon its knights and lords.
You must accept what fate decrees; proceed
Exactly as the shah commands you to.
Bind on the shackles now, with your own hands.
There is no shame in royal bonds, and when
I take you shackled to the shah, if there's
A crime, it will be on his head alone.
These fetters wound my heart as well. I vow,
As I am standing face to face with you,
To set you free before the day is done.
Nor will I let you suffer any harm.
Believe me when I say, great pahlavān,
You won't be wronged by this fair-minded shah.
Later, when I have set the crown upon
My head, I'll place the whole world in your hands.
In this way neither will there be a crime
In Yazdān's eyes nor shame for me before
The shah. In spring, the time of blossoming,
When you next see Zābolestān, you will
Receive vast treasures from my hands. By these
Your lands will be made beautiful as well."
Rostam replied, "O famous shah, I've prayed
For many years to our Creator that
One day I'd have the joy of seeing you.
I've seen you now and seen the pain you'll cause.

We are two heroes, you and I, one young,
One old—both shrewd and able pahlavāns.
I fear the evil eye will strike one day
And wake you from your pleasant dream.
The demon always finds his way inside
And twists the heart toward a crown and throne.
I know some shame will come to me from this
That won't be worn away by passing years.
It's clear that you, the army's noblest chief,
A proud, renowned and lionhearted prince,
Won't deign to visit in my home, will not,
In my own homeland, be my guest.
If you will rid your mind of haughty thoughts,
And strive to exorcise this demon's rule,
I'll look upon your face with joyful heart
And gladly do whatever you command.
But not these chains. Shackles are shame, defeat,
An ugly stain upon my family's name.
While I'm alive, no one will ever see
Me bound with chains. My soul insists on this.
I've fought with many warriors 'till now.
But none has had the strength to shackle me."
Esfandiyār replied, "Exemplar of
The world's great paladins! You've spoken truth.
You have not lied. We men of worth are not
Attracted by such crookedness. And yet
My brother, Pashutan, has witnessed what
The shah commanded when I left the court.
If I approach your palace now and so,
Triumphant, enter as a happy guest,
And you in turn defy the shah's command,

My shining day will turn as black as pitch.
What's more, if after that I should forget
This bread and salt, and like a raging leopard
Attack you on the field, my fortune will
Be changed as well. If now, like you, I should
Ignore the shah's command, I know my place
Within the other world will be the fire.
Suppose your wish should be fulfilled and we,
In company, raise high a cup of wine.
What will tomorrow bring? What man can say?
Of this it's better not to speak at all."
"I'll leave you now," Rostam replied, "to change
These dusty clothes. I have been hunting for
A week and dining on roast onager
Instead of lamb. Once you are seated with
Your intimates, and it is time to eat,
Call for me then." He mounted Rakhsh from where
He stood, his wounded heart immersed in thought,
And galloped 'til he reached the palace gates.
He saw his father, Zāl, descendant of
The heroes Sām and Narimān, and said
To him, "O noble lord! I've been to see
Esfandiyār and met him seated on
His horse, as stately as a cypress tree.
Adorned with kingly radiance, and wise.
It seemed that Feraydun had given him
His grandeur and his wisdom as a gift.
He radiated majesty and was
Himself far greater than he's been described.'

When Rostam turned and left the stream, the shah
Was filled with anxious thoughts. His counselor,
Brave Pashutan, arrived just then within
The palace tent. His valiant brother turned
And spoke, "We thought this was an easy task,
But it's proved hard indeed. I have no wish
To visit Rostam in his home, nor has
He any need to see me here. Should he
Not choose to come, I will not send for him.
If one of us should breathe his last while here,
His death will sear the heart of him who's left.
A closer friendship would increase that grief."
Brave Pashutan replied, "Where could one find
A brother like Esfandiyār? By glorious
Yazdān, when I first saw Esfandiyār
And Tahamtan, two warlike pahlavāns,
Had met, but did not wish to fight, my heart
Rejoiced like spring for both of you.
But when I looked again, I saw a div
Who blocks the way where judgment leads. You are
Devout and wise, your soul's been nurtured on
Sagacity as well. I beg you now,
Hear this advice your brother gives. Proceed
With utmost care. Don't war with your own soul!
I heard each word that Rostam spoke and how
His greatness joined with manliness in what
He said. Your bonds will never chafe his legs.
He will not yield himself so easily.
This world-famed cavalier, this seed of Zāl
And Sām, won't let himself be captured by

Some clever ruse. Among the heroes of
The world there's none so shrewd and skilled as he.
How could one hobble Rostam's legs? And why?
Don't threaten what will never be. For one
Who is a valiant knight to utter such
Unworthy, vicious words cannot be right.
You are both pahlavāns and so I fear
This ugly quarrel will go on too long.
You know far more than Shah Goshtāsp, and are
More brave and manly too. Rostam bids you
To feast. Goshtāsp provokes your enmity.
Tell me, which of these two deserves your praise?"
His brother, glorious Esfandiyār
Replied, "Should I ignore the shah's command,
I will be censured in this world, and in
The next I'll surely face the judgment of Izad.
I will not lose both worlds to win Rostam.
There is no way to hide my acts from God."
His brother said, "Whatever counsel might
Be useful to your body and your soul,
I've spoken it. You choose what's right. The hearts
Of shahs do not incline to war and vengeance."
Esfandiyār commanded that the cooks
Bring out the feast but called no one to dine.
When he was done, he took a cup of wine
And spoke with Pashutan about the Fort
Of Brass* and his adventures there, then drank
A cup to honor Shah Goshtāsp. Meanwhile
Rostam was seated in his hall. He kept
His word and did not eat. Some time went by;
No messenger appeared as he sat there,

---

* Arjāsp's capital city which was surrounded by an impenetrable wall

His eyes upon the road. But when the time
For food had passed, his patience overflowed.
He laughed and said to Zavāreh, "You have
Them serve the feast, and bid the nobles come.
It seems this is the custom of the gallant
Esfandiyār. Remember it!" He sent
For them to saddle Rakhsh and ornament
His saddle in the Chinese way. "I'll call
Upon Esfandiyār once more," he said.
"I will not be dismissed so easily."

I AM THE GUARDIAN OF IRAN (575–623)

He mounted Rakhsh, and seized his ox head mace,
Then like a maddened elephant, he rode
Toward the Hirmand's bank. The soldiers of
The shah all hastened to observe him as
He rode. The hearts of those who saw him there
Were filled with loyalty and love for him
Each one remarked, "This worthy pahlavān
Can only be compared to Sām. Look how
He sits his saddle like a hill of iron,
And Rakhsh himself you'd say was Ahriman.
If now an elephant should charge, he'd set
A Nile of blood to flowing from its skull.
In all the world, no one has ever seen
A man like this nor heard of one from times
Long past. What can Goshtāsp be thinking of
To send his son to battle with this knight?
To keep the crown within his hands, he'll send
A peerless hero to a certain death.
In his old age he's grown more covetous

Of wealth, more proud of seal and diadem."
While from afar Rostam came galloping
Astride the fire-breathing Rakhsh. As he
Approached the camp of the Iranians
Esfandiyār came out to welcome him.
Rostam saluted him: "O happy youth!
New branch upon the Best of Faiths.* It seems
These new beliefs have changed your customs, too,
And you no longer bid your guests to dine.
Hear what I say! Beware of challenging
This ancient knight unless you have sound cause.
You so esteem yourself and so admire
Your courtiers, you slight my manliness
And think me neither wise nor shrewd. But in
This world I am Rostam, the glorious seed
Of Sām and Narimān. The White Div bites
His claw from fear of me. Magicians I
Make vanish by the score. Great warriors
Have seen my tiger skin upon the field
And seen this roaring lion, Rakhsh, as well.
In battle once I snatched first Kāmus† then
The Chinese Khāqān from their saddles with
My rope, though both were famous for their strength
And bravery, then bound them hand and foot.
I am the guardian of Iran, and of
Its heroes, too—their firm support and guide
In every war. Do not distrust this offer,
Nor think that you stand higher than the heavens.
Acknowledging your royal grace and state,
I've sought your counsel and some tie
With you. I do not want a shah like you

---

* Zoroastrianism
† A Turānian lord who attacked Iran during the reign of Kay Khosrow

To be destroyed by fighting me one day.
The hero Sām was bravery itself,
Male lions fled their lairs at his approach.
In this world now I am his heir. What's more,
Heroic shah Esfandiyār, I have,
For many years, been known as pahlavān
Of all the world and often praised. I thank
Yazdān that he has given me long life
So I might see a shah who is my peer,
Who visits vengeance on the infidels
And wins thereby the praise of all the world.
You are a famous, noble warrior,
The crown of heroes on the battlefield."
Esfandiyār smiled at Rostam and said,
"Oh grandson of the horseman Sām. You are
Upset because I sent no invitation.
I did not mean to raise myself above
You by this act. The day was hot, the way
Was long, I did not wish to trouble you.
Don't be offended by this slight, or speak
So angrily. I said "At dawn tomorrow,
I'll find some way to make amends. I'll ride
Off cheerfully to greet Dastān and spend
A pleasant hour with Rostam. But now,
You've left your home to cross the desert to
Our camp, and so distressed yourself instead.
Come, sit with us awhile and raise a cup,
Don't speak such harsh and quarellsome words."
He made a space at his left hand and bid
Him sit beside him there. "That's not my place,"
The seasoned knight replied. "I'll choose the seat

That is my due. Bahman," he said, "prepare
A seat at his right hand, one suitable
For me." And then, enraged, he told the prince,
"Open your eyes, and look at me! See here
My prowess and my celebrated name.
I am the seed of warlike Sām. A man
Who's worthy has an open hand. His heart's
Imbued with justice, too. His value comes
From valor, dignity and noble birth. If you've
No place appropriate for me, I still
Retain my honor, name and dignity."
When he was done, the shah commanded that
His son provide a golden chair and place
It so the valiant pahlavān might sit
At ease. Still filled with rage, Tahamtan took
His seat beside the youthful shahriyār,
A fragrant citron clasped within his hand.

THIS BASE BORN OFFSPRING OF SOME DIV (624–643)

Esfandiyār addressed Rostam and said,
"Illustrious and famous knight! I've heard
From sages, nobles, learned priests, and from
Your pious ancestors as well, that Zāl,
This baseborn offspring of some div, is not
Descended from a human sire. When he
Was born his face and head were snowy white,
His body black as pitch. For days they hid
His birth from Sām, believing it to be
A fearful omen of the Day of Judgment.
Poor Sām! He looked upon his newborn son
And knew despair. He ordered them

To throw this child into the sea where he
Would be devoured by fish and birds. Simorgh[*]
Flew down, and hovered there above the child,
But saw no sign of grace or strength in him.
She carried Zāl up to her nest, planning
To make a meal of him. But there, although
The bird was ravenous, she found the child
Inedible and drove him from her nest.
No one, it seems, was pleased to see this child.
He fed his naked, feeble body on
The scraps of food she threw him from the nest.
At last, she felt a kindliness toward him.
Some time went by. The heavens turned above.
When he had fattened on her scraps awhile,
She brought him naked to Sistān. Once there,
Poor, childless Sām, whom age had made both weak
And foolish, took him in. The generous lords
And radiant shahs, who are my ancestors,
Raised up this child and gave him lands and wealth.
In this way many years went by. Zāl grew
Into a tall and stately cypress tree,
Whose top no one could reach. Then he
Put forth a branch and fruit—the child, Rostam,
Who by his strength, great size and manliness
Increased his wealth and state. Now this
Prosperity has turned his thoughts away
From righteousness and loyalty, and he
Desires to rule as though he were the shah."

WHO HAS A NOBLER ANCESTRY THAN THIS? (644–683)

Rostam replied, "Compose yourself. Why speak

---

[*] The magical bird who adopted Zāl and raised him in her nest after his father abandoned him

To me in such insulting terms? Your heart
Exudes foul humors, and it seems your soul's
Been tutored by some div. Speak as befits
A royal prince, and only say what's true.
The Lord of all the World knows that Dastān,
The son of Sām, is wise and great, and has
An honored name. And Sām, a hero of
The noblest stock, was born to Narimān.
His father was the great Garshāsp, a shah
Whose fame filled all the world. You've heard, I'm sure,
Accounts of Sām. In his own day no one
Could equal his renown. In Tus he slew
A fearsome dragon once, with claws that none
Escaped. Sām was a crocodile at sea,
A leopard on dry ground. Who ever saw
Him turn and flee the battlefield? Within
The sea he singed the fishes' skulls and scorched
The wings of vultures in midair. He drew
An elephant to him, the very thought
Of whom would make a joyful heart despair,
By simply drawing in his breath. There was
An evil-tempered div as well, whose head
Reached to the sky. The hot sun scorched his brow,
And yet the Sea of China only broke
Against this monster's waist. He plucked fish from
The sea, then standing with his head above
The moon he broiled them on the sun. From fear
Of him the turning heavens wept. Two grave
Afflictions such as these were threatening
Until the both of them were slain by Sām's
Heroic sword. My mother, Rudābeh,

Was born the daughter of Mehrāb, who ruled
All Hend both long and well. The fifth in line
From Shah Zahhāk, he was a shah who stood
Above the other monarchs of the world.
Who has a nobler ancestry than this?
A man who's wise will not deny the truth.
What's more, throughout the world, a hero who
Would know what virtue is must find it here—
In me. I first received the deed of rule
From Shah Kāvus. No one can fault me there.
Shah Kay Khosrow the Just renewed the deed.
Among the shahs who've worn the royal belt
There's none like him. I've journeyed through the land
From end to end; slain many unjust shahs.
I forded Jayhun's flood, marched through Turān
And chased Afrāsiyāb to China's sea.
Recall Hāmāvarān and Kay Kāvus,
My journey to Māzandarān as well.
No demon there escaped me with his life.
I slew White Div—Arzhang, Pulād Ghandi,
Sanjeh and Beed as well.* In order to
Protect the shah I killed my son, my wise
Courageous son. For strength and martial skill
There's never been a hero like Sohrāb.
It's been five hundred years, or more, since I
Was born to Zāl. And all that time I've been
A pahlavān within this world. Like Feraydun
Of glorious descent, who placed the crown
Of greatness on his head, dethroned Zahhāk
And brought him and his crown to dust, my words
And deeds have been as one. Next, Sām,

---

* Rostam's battles in Māzandarān with the White Div and these other
named demons occur in the first section of the reign of Kay Kāvus.

Who was my grandfather, had mastered all
The crafts and learning of this world. And third,
Since I first armed myself, all those who wear
A crown have lived at ease. There's never been
A time of joy and happiness like this.
Rebellious chiefs have been denied the court
Because of all the battles I have fought
And victories I have won. The heavy mace
And sword belong to me. I've told you this
Because you are a shah, these warriors
Are like your flock and follow you. You've come
Into this world quite recently, and so,
Although you have the aura of a shah,
Your thoughts are of yourself alone. You still
Are blind to other, hidden things. But come,
Enough of words like these. Let's raise a cup,
And so annihilate our cares with wine."

I AM DESCENDED FROM GOSHTASP, THE SHAH (684–725)

On hearing Rostam's words, Esfandiyār
Rejoiced. His heart beat faster, and
He said, "The difficulties you've endured,
The victories you've won, I've heard them all.
Now I'll recount what I have done to raise
Myself above the heroes of the world.
At first I took up arms to serve the faith,
To cleanse the earth of idol worshipers.
In all the world, no one's seen battles such
As these—so many bodies that they hid
The earth from view. I am descended from
Goshtāsp, the shah, and he from Shah Lohrāsp.

Lohrāsp, in turn, was son to Owrand Shah,
Whose family was the senior royal line.
He was the son of Kay Pashin, who blessed
The infant Owrand at his birth. Pashin's
The seed of Kay Qobād, a shah both wise
And just. You can pursue my ancestry
In just this way to Feraydun, the shah
Who ruled the world and was the ornament
Of his own age. What's more, my mother was
The child of Caesar, the crown adorning all
The Roman state. He traces his descent
To Salm, and so, again, to Feraydun
The Just and Glorious. Salm was the son
Of Feraydun the Valiant, who seized
The title shah from all who claimed to rule.
This I will say, and none deny, though lies
Are many, and truth is rare, both you and Sām
Were servants to my royal ancestors,
Those noble shahs of pure descent. This is
The simple truth. Your greatness is a gift
From them, and it is yours because you served
Them zealously and well. I'll tell you all
My story now, and if a single word's
Untrue, point out the lie. Since first Goshtāsp
Received the throne, I have been armed by fortune
And by manliness. I am the one who spread
The faith as far as China and whom
All praised for this. Then later on, because
Of lies Gorazm told, my father had
Me bound and exiled from the court. These bonds
Caused Lohrāsp's death, for Turān's troops soon hid

Iran beneath their marching feet. Jāmāsp,
My father's counselor, brought blacksmiths to
My cell to free me from these heavy chains.
But they worked slowly. My heart longed for
A sword and was oppressed by care. I freed
My body from the blacksmiths' hands, stood up
And shattered bolts and chains with my own strength.
At my approach Shah Arjāsp turned and fled,
The Turānian nobility as well.
I armed myself with valor and pursued
That host, a raging lion after prey.
You've heard how in my seven labors I
Was attacked by lions and by Ahriman;
And how, by using guile, I entered the Fort
Of Brass, demolished all within and so
Avenged the nobles of Iran, whose blood
Turānians had shed. No onager
Beneath the leopard's claws, no crocodile
Who feels the seaman's hook has suffered as
I did while in Turān and China, and yet
No one's accomplished more than I have done.
From the days of Tur and valiant Feraydun,
No one has mentioned this fort's name. It's black
And stands atop a mountain peak, whose height
Sequesters it from all the throngs of men.
When I arrived, they worshiped idols there
And wandered drunkenly, as in a daze.
By my own bravery I breached its walls,
Threw all its idols down, and in their place
I lit the flame that Zarātosht* first brought
From heaven in a sacred dish. Then with

---

* Zoroaster, the prophet of the religion that bears his name

The victories the just and only God
Had given me, I rode back to Iran.
Our enemies were routed everywhere.
No Brahmin* prayed within his temple's walls.
In all my battles I have fought alone.
None shared with me the care and pain of war.
But we have surely had enough of words;
If you are thirsty, raise your cup and drink."

HIGH HEAVEN WILL NOT BIND
THESE HANDS OF MINE! (726–787)

Rostam replied to him, "Our deeds remain
As our memorial. Be just, and hear
The words this old but famous warrior
Now says to you. Had I not journeyed with
My ox head mace to far Māzandarān,
Where Kāvus Shah, together with both Giv
And Tus,† had been made captive and the sound
Of war drums split the ear, who would have crushed
The White Div's heart and brain? Who else was there
Who trusted in his arm that much? I killed
The sorcerers as well—cut off their heads, and left
Their bodies there with neither shroud nor grave—
Then loosed the bonds that held the shah and bore
Him to the throne. The people of Iran
Rejoiced in him, and he in fortune's smile.
My only allies in my seven labors
Were Rakhsh and this sharp sword that gives
The world to whom it will. When Kay Kāvus
Had journeyed to Hāmāvarān, and was
Made prisoner, I raised an army from

---

* Hindu religious caste
† Giv and Tus were notables in Kay Kāvus's court.

77

The lords and nobles of Iran, and led
Them off to war. I slew their shah in battle,
Laying waste that famous throne. Shah Kay
Kāvus, the ruler of the world, was bound
In chains, and burdened by great pain and grief.
I freed him from his bonds, bold Giv, Gudarz*
And Tus as well. Meanwhile, Afrāsiyāb,
With all his evil guard, had overrun
Iran, filling the world with his foul deeds.
I led our boundless army and the shah
Home to Iran. Alone, I raced ahead
By night, seeking not my ease but fame.
When he first spied my standard flying on
The wind, and heard Rakhsh neigh, Afrāsiyāb
Turned tail and fled to China's court. Once more
The world was filled with justice and with praise.
If blood had flowed from Kay Kāvus's throat,
How then could Seyāvash have followed him
Or sired the chaste and gallant Kay Khosrow,
Who left his throne to Shah Lohrāsp in turn?
Within this court, my father, Zāl, a brave
And worthy man, bowed to Lohrāsp and called
Him shah, the dust of shame within his mouth—
To honor one with neither name nor fame.
Why should you boast of Goshtāsp's crown,
Or that of newly royal Shah Lohrāsp?
Who tells you, 'Go and shackle Rostam's hands!'
High heaven will not bind these hands of mine!
If it should say to me, 'Obey him now,'
I'd raise my mace and box its ears. Since I
Was just a child 'til now when I've grown old,

---

* Gudarz is another notable in Kay Kāvus's court.

I've never borne such words from any man.
I would be shamed to plead my case or beg
For help. Such gentle words diminish me."
Esfandiyār burst into laughter at
Rostam's ferocity. He firmly grasped
His hand and said, "Rostam, Tahamtan, you are
Exactly as I've heard from everyone.
Your arm seems massive as a lion's thigh,
Especially when you take your mace in hand.
You have a dragon's chest and shoulders, and
Your waist is slender as a hunting leopard's."
But as he talked, he crushed his hand within
His own. The aged hero smiled at him.
He did not flinch with pain, though yellow bile
Poured from his fingernails. Then Rostam seized
The hand of his superior and said,
"Great shah, and pious servant of Yazdān!
Far-famed Goshtāsp is fortunate to have
A son like you, and fortunate is she
Who bears a son like bold Esfandiyār.
Her worldly luster grows with every day."
While Rostam spoke, he crushed the young man's hand
Within his fist. The prince's face turned red
As blood. His nails ran red with blood as well,
While pain creased all his brow. Yet fortunate
Esfandiyār laughed at Rostam and said,
"Enjoy your wine today, famed Tahamtan!
Tomorrow on the battlefield, your thoughts will be
Of pain and strife, and not this pleasant feast.
I'll place my golden saddle on my jet-
Black horse, tie on my royal casque. Then with

My lance, I'll stretch you on the ground. When I've
Done that, you'll think no more rebellious thoughts.
I'll bind your hands, convey you to the shah
And say I find you innocent of wrong.
We'll humbly plead your case and find, at last,
A resolution that's both just and fair.
We'll free you from all care and grief;
Your suffering will have its just reward."
Then Rostam laughed in turn and said to brave
Esfandiyār, "You'll soon grow weary of
The battlefield. What do you know of men
At war; when have you felt the mace's breath
Upon your cheek? If heaven should prove fickle,
And turn its kindest face away from us,
Instead of wine we'll taste red death; we'll know
The pain of ambush, feel the lasso's grip
And hear the sound of war drums, not of lutes.
Our greetings and farewells will be the blows
Of heavy mace and sword. O fortunate
Esfandiyār, you wish to know which way
This war will go? Tomorrow when you ride
Onto the battlefield, and we fight man
To man, I'll seize you from your horse in my
Strong grip and carry you to Zāl, then seat
You on his ivory throne and place upon
Your head a glorious crown that Kay Qobād,
Whose soul rejoices now in Paradise,
Once gave to me. I'll open wide the doors
Of all my treasuries, heap riches at
Your feet and make your army wealthy past
All need. I'll raise your royal crown up to

The highest heaven. After that, we'll set
Out riding to the royal court, and make
Our journey light with laughter and good cheer.
I'll boldly place the crown upon your head
To show my thanks to Shah Goshtāsp, then bind
The belt of servitude around my waist,
As I have done for other shahs. I'll weed
The garden of Iran from end to end
And so renew myself as though newborn.
When you are shah, and I am pahlavān,
No enemy will live to draw a breath."

DO NOT, GREAT SHAH,
TORMENT OUR HEARTS THIS WAY! (788–879)

Esfandiyār replied to him, "To go
On speaking now would be of little use.
We're hungry and the day's half gone. We've talked
Enough of war, time now to feast. Tell them
To bring our food and not invite those who
Will talk too much." When they had served the food,
Rostam began to eat. Those standing there
Looked on in awe to see him feast. The prince,
Esfandiyār, and others of his court,
Brought roasted lamb to him from every side.
The lord commanded them, "Bring him a cup,
And fill it up with wine that's raw, not cooked.
Let's see what Rostam says when he is in
His cups and how he speaks of Kay Kāvus."
The steward brought a cup of wine—a cup
In which one might have set a ship afloat.
Toasting the health of the shāhanshāh,

He drained the cup down to its golden lees.
The youthful page filled up the cup once more
With a vintage worthy of a shah. Rostam
Said privately to Pashutan, "Your wine
Does not require that you dilute it much.
When you pour water in the cup you break
The vigor of old wine." So Pashutan
Ordered the serving boy to pour raw wine
Into a cup and bring it to Rostam. He called
For minstrels, too, then watched astonished as
Tahamtan drank it off. When it was time
To leave, his face was flushed with wine.
Esfandiyār bid him farewell: "May you
Be happy for as long as time endures.
May you be nourished by this food and drink,
And may your soul be strengthened, too." Rostam
Replied, "Great shah, may wisdom always be
Your guide. Whatever wine I've drunk with you
Has nourished me and strengthened reason in
My soul as well. If you will free your mind
Of enmity, you'll choose the wiser way.
You'll leave the plain and come into my home
And, happily, you'll be my guest awhile.
Judgment will be my guide as well, and I'll
Fulfill the promises I've made. Rest for
Some days; don't strive to do what's wrong. Show your
Humanity and common sense instead."
Esfandiyār, the hero, answered him:
"Don't plant a seed that will not grow. Tomorrow,
When I have armed myself for war, you'll see
At last what brave and noble men can do.

Don't praise your body's strength. Go home. Prepare
Instead to face the coming day. You'll learn
That I'm as much at home upon the field
Of war, as I am here with cups and wine.
When I depart Zābol and reach Iran,
I'll go before the shah and all the court.
You'll see my actions there will far exceed
My words. Don't try to cause me grief in this."
Tahamtan's heart grew heavy at these words,
The world seemed like a thicket, dark and dense.
"Whether I let him bind my legs and arms,"
He thought, "or boldly choose to do him harm,
Both actions lead to evil and disgrace.
To set such harmful precedents is wrong.
His shackles will disgrace my name, and Shah
Goshtāsp will do me harm at last. Throughout
The world, whoever has the power of speech
Will never weary of reproaching me.
'Rostam was beaten by a single youth,
Who entered Kābol, bound his arms and brought
Him to Iran.' My name will be disgraced.
No scent or hue of Rostam will survive.
And if he's slain upon the battlefield,
His death will shame me in all royal eyes.
'He slew the youthful shah,' they'll say, 'because
His speech to him was impolite and harsh.'
For this, when I am dead, I will be cursed
By all, and called an infidel. If I,
Instead, am killed by him, Zābol itself
Will lose all name and fame. No one will speak
Of it with pride. The names of Zāl and Sām

Will be forgotten, too. And yet, perhaps,
My words of praise will be repeated still."
To glorious Esfandiyār, he said,
"My face grows pale as I reflect on this.
You speak so much of shackling me. Your bonds
And wishes both are wounds to me. Perhaps
The writ of heaven runs another way.
The turning sphere is far above our own
Imaginings. You heed advice from divs,
But will not hear the counsel of the wise.
The years you've lived are few. You do not see
The shah's malicious tricks. Your heart is pure,
And you know nothing of the world. Meanwhile,
The shah in secret plots your death. Goshtāsp
Will never weary of the crown and throne.
They're in his stars. That's why he sends you off
Adventuring around the world and thrusts
You into each new crisis he stirs up. He searched
The earth from end to end, his clever mind
As sharp as any ax or adz, to find
Some hero who had never turned aside
From bloody strife and who was strong enough
To do you harm. All this so this high throne
And crown would stay within his grasp. It would
Be right for us to curse the throne. Should we,
To serve his purpose, make the earth our bed?
You heap chastisement on my soul. You should,
Instead, consider what you're doing here.
With your own hand you sow misfortune for
Yourself and harvest only enmity.
O shah! Do not do this! Don't blithely court

Disaster as though you were a thoughtless boy.
Do not, great shah, torment our hearts this way.
Don't bring affliction down upon your soul.
Humble yourself before Yazdān, and show
Respect to me. Do not betray yourself
This way. You have no need to war with me—
To launch attacks and strive against me now.
It's destiny that drives you here with troops
And arms, to be destroyed by me. For this,
I know I'll leave behind a shameful name.
May Goshtāsp's name decline as mine has done!"
When proud Esfandiyār heard his reply
He answered him: "O famous Tahamtan,
Consider what a former sage once said,
When wisdom filled his soul. 'However much
An old man knows, however great his triumphs,
If he proves false, he is a fool.' You practice
Your deceits on me to free your shoulders of
This heavy yoke. You wish that all who hear
This tale will think these handsome words of yours
Are true. That I, whose thoughts are pure, they'll call
Malignant and untrue, while you they'll think
A man who's both intelligent and good. They'll say,
'Esfandiyār at first spoke graciously,
Inviting him to feast, and so raised up
The hopes of Tahamtan, who only spurned
His words when he found nothing there but strife.
Esfandiyār rejected all his pleas
And spoke to him in bitter terms.' Hear me!
I will not disobey the shah's command,
Not for a crown or throne. I find in him

Whatever's good or evil in this world.
My hell and heaven are contained in him.
May you be strengthened by whatever you
Have eaten here, and may it injure all
Your enemies. Go home in safety now;
Report to Zāl what you have seen and heard.
Ready your weapons for the coming fight,
And speak to me no more in words. At dawn
Ride out prepared to fight. Do not prolong
This matter for yourself. Tomorrow on
The field of war, the world before your eyes
Will turn to night. Then you will learn
How men of virtue fight upon the day
That ends in victory or shame." Rostam
Replied to him: "O lionhearted shah!
If this is your desire, I'll treat you to
The sight of Rakhsh's charge, and with my mace
I'll cure your headache, too. In your own court
You've heard, and you've believed it, every word,
That on the battlefield, the swords of heroes
Are powerless against Esfandiyār.
Tomorrow you will see my lance's point,
And Rakhsh's reins within my grip. Hereafter,
You'll never wish to challenge any hero
Or fight upon the battlefield." A smile
That humbled pearls formed on the young man's lips.
He spoke to Rostam, saying, "You are so keen
For fame, why has our talk here angered you?
Tomorrow on the plain you'll see how men
Of strength and virtue fight. Is it not true
That I'm a mountain peak and that my horse

Is like a mountain, too? I am one man
But like a company upon the field.
And should your mother, brokenhearted, weep
Because you felt my mace's wind upon
Your brow, that is, if you are slain in battle,
I'll tie you to your horse, and lead you to
The court. Henceforth, no servant of the shah
Will challenge him upon the field of war."

I'LL MAKE HIS SHINING DAY AS DARK AS NIGHT (880–930)

As Rostam rose to leave the prince's camp,
He paused a moment by the door and turned
To speak directly to the royal tent.
"O Palace of Hope!" he said. "Happy the time
When you were home to Shah Jamshid! And blessed
The days of Kay Kāvus and Kay Khosrow
The Glorious! Because the man who sits
Upon the throne does not deserve to rule,
The gates of fortune now are closed to you."
Hearing these words, the bold Esfandiyār
Descended from his throne and strode toward
Rostam. "O proud and wilful man! Why are
You quarreling with my tent? Zābol should be
Renamed the Land of Wild and Foolish Talk.
Here, when a guest grows weary of his host,
He turns to insults and disparages
His name." Turning to the royal tent, he said,
"There was a time when you embraced Jamshid,
A time as well when Kay Kāvus held court
Within these walls and found his refuge here.
How did he follow Yazdān's way? He longed

To hold the stars within his hands and filled
The world with strife—with clubs and knives and war.
The one who rules here now is Goshtāsp Shah-
His counselor is wise Jāmāsp, and by
His side sits Zarātosht, who brought the *Zand
Avesta** down to us from Paradise.
At Goshtāsp's other side sits Pashutan
The brave and good, who's tasted both the sweet
And bitter of this world. And standing there
As well, Esfandiyār the fortunate,
By whom the turning heavens are rejoiced.
Good men take heart from him. The wicked fear
His sword which subjugates them one and all."
Rostam strode to the door, mounted Rakhsh and left.
Esfandiyār observed him as he went,
Then turned to Pashutan. "Such manliness
And heroism cannot be concealed.
I've never seen a horse or horseman such
As Tahamtan and Rakhsh. If we must fight
I do not know how he will fare. When he
Is armed and ready for the fray, he's like
A raging elephant astride Mt. Gang.
Dressed in his armor and his arms, he's the
Embodiment of manliness and strength.
His height exceeds all grace and comeliness,
And yet, I fear, tomorrow he will know
Defeat. My heart is drawn toward that splendor,
But I will not sever it from God's decree.
When he confronts me on the field of war,
I'll make his shining day as dark as night."
Wise Pashutan replied, "My brother, hear

---

* The sacred book of Zoroastrianism

88

Me out. Do not do this. I've said to you
Before, and say again, because I will
Not ever purge my heart of truth, do not
Torment this man. A noble heart will not
Submit from injury or pain. Sleep well
Tonight. Tomorrow, just at dawn, ride off
With neither troops nor guards to Rostam's palace.
There let us spend a cheerful time with him
And answer every question he may raise.
What he has done within the world, whether
Among the nobles or the commoners,
Has all been good. I see him loyal to
His bond with you. He will not disregard
What you demand of him. Why speak to him
So angrily? Empty your heart of vengeance,
And cleanse your eyes of wrath." Esfandiyār
Replied, "A thorn has taken root within
The garden here. A pious man," he said,
"Should never speak as you have done. You are
Vizier of all Iran—the eyes and ears,
The very heart of its brave men. And yet
You recommend a course like this and say
It's wise to vex the shah! All I have done,
The pains that I've endured,have vanished like
The wind. The faith of Zarātosht, which says
That he who turns his back upon the shah
Will end in hell, is now proved wrong. How long
Will you encourage me to sin and urge
Me to rebel against the shah. These are
Your words. Yet how shall I do that when I
Have sworn obedience to Shāh Goshtāsp?

You're fearful I'll be killed or wounded in
This fight. Today I'll break you of that fear.
In all the world no one has died except
At his appointed hour. And he who's gained
A name for bravery will never die.
Tomorrow on the battlefield you'll see
What I can do against this fearsome leopard!"
"My famous brother," Pashutan replied,
"Why are you speaking now of war and strife?
Since you first armed yourself with bow and arrow,
Eblis has had no hold upon your thoughts.
Now you have welcomed him into your heart
And will not hear my counsel and advice.
I see your heart's confused—filled with a rage
That scatters all my words. How shall I free
My heart of fear; how can I put aside
My anxious thoughts? I see two lions,
Two brave, ferocious pahlavāns. How can
I know which one will triumph, which taste defeat?"
Esfandiyār did not reply. His heart
Was filled with pain, his mind with windy pride.

I READ THE BOOK OF SERVITUDE TO HIM (931–992)

Within his palace, Rostam paused a moment
To read the register of warriors
Who'd served with him. His brother, Zavāreh,
Approached, and saw him weary, pale and sad.
"Go, bring an Indian sword," he said, "a shirt
Of mail and helmet, too. Bring me a rope,
A suit of armor and my tiger skin.
Bring shield and heavy mace, and bow as well."

So Zavāreh commanded the keeper of
The treasury to bring what he required.
When Rostam saw his weapons there, he bowed
His head and sighed, "O famous tiger skin,
You've rested for a while from war, now there
Is work for you once more. Be strong, and be
My lucky shirt wherever I may go.
There is a battlefield, where two male lions,
Both brave and powerful, will meet at last.
I wonder how Esfandiyār will fight—
What tricks he'll try on me when we two meet."
When Dastān heard Tahamtan's words, the old
Man's soul was filled with care. He said to him,
"O famous pahlavān, what's this you say?
My soul's grown dark on hearing it. Since you
First mounted up to ride to war, you've been
Both resolute and bold, unburdened by
Your cares and proud to serve the shah.
I fear your day has reached its end or that
Your lucky star is sleeping. Now they'll uproot
The seed of Dastān's line, annihilate
His wives and children, too, should you be slain
In battle by this youth, Esfandiyār.
Zābol will perish, too—its lands laid waste,
Its rivers drained, its lofty heights brought low.
But if, instead, Esfandiyār should die,
It's you, Rostam, who'll lose your honored name.
They'll tell this story everywhere—abase
The name that you have raised so high: 'Because
A youthful prince of Goshtāsp's line once spoke
To him discourteously, he struck him down.'

Go, stand and wait before him now. Or if
You won't, then flee at once. Take refuge in
Some unknown place, remote from wellborn men.
This dreadful act will darken all your soul.
Shun battle with this youthful prince. Buy back
Your soul with gifts and loyal service. Now is
The time for Chinese silks, not mace and shield.
Adorn his army with brocaded robes.
Purchase yourself from him with precious goods.
When he departs the Hirmand's bank, mount Rakhsh
And, safe once more, ride humbly at his side.
Obey his orders on the road until
You reach the court and stand before the shah.
Once you are there, will Goshtāsp do you harm?
Such shameful acts do not befit a shah."
Rostam replied, "Father, do not dismiss
So easily these words I speak. I've been
A hero now for many years, and I've
Endured both good and evil in that time.
I faced the demons of Māzandarān,
The horsemen of Hāmāvarān as well.
The earth trembled beneath the Chinese khan
And fierce Kāmus. I slew them both. If I
Should flee Esfandiyār, you must give up
The palaces and gardens of Sistān.
When, in my tiger skin, I go to war,
I bring the sun and moon down to the earth.
These stratagems of yours, I've tried them all.
I read the book of servitude to him.
He mocked my words. He slights my wisdom and
My counsel, too. If he'd descend to earth

From Saturn's sphere and welcome me within
His soul, there's nothing I'd withhold from him,
No wealth or treasure, no armor, mace or sword.
We've spoken many words, met several times;
From all this talk the wind alone remains.
Tomorrow, if he should choose to fight with me,
Do not be fearful for his life. I won't
Chase after him to fight, nor will he see
My mace or lance's point. I'll block his way
As he rides out to fight, seize him firmly
Around the waist, and lift him from his horse,
Then raise him high above Goshtāsp as shah.
That is, I'll bring him here, seat him upon
A throne and open wide the treasury's doors.
When he has been my guest for three full days,
Upon the fourth, when the world-illuming sun
Strikes down the Nile blue tent of night, and in
The cup of day, the golden gem appears,
I'll pledge myself to him, then take the road
To Goshtāsp's court. I'll seat Esfandiyār
Upon the famous ivory throne and place
Upon his head that crown that lights all hearts.
I'll pledge myself to him obediently
And swear to serve forever at his side.
You know how in Shah Qobād's time I served
The throne courageously. Recall that now."
The golden Zāl laughed at his words and shook
His head in grave perplexity: "Oh, son!"
He said to him. "Don't speak such words. Cut off
Their heads, and let them die. If madmen were
To hear these words of yours, they'd think

Them raw and foolish, too. You're like Qobād
Seated off someplace alone and sad,
No throne or crown, no treasury. Do not
Compare yourself to Shah Esfandiyār—
Who has authority and ancient wealth, and leads
The army of Iran. China's Faghfur*
Inscribes his name upon his seal. You say,
'I'll lift him off his horse and bring him to
The Palace of Dastān.' A man who's ripe
With years would never speak like this. Do not
Approach the threshold of ingratitude."
He spoke, then bowed his forehead to the ground
And praised the Maker of the World. "Just Lord!
I pray that You will turn the evil of
This day away from us." Zāl did not cease
From prayer 'til the sun rose up at dawn.

FORTUNE FAVORS THE MAN WHO'S JUST (993–1054)

When it was day, Rostam put on a coat
Of mail and tiger skin to shield himself,
Tied a lasso to his saddle ring
And mounted elephantine Rakhsh.
He called for Zavāreh, who stood nearby,
And gave him orders for the coming day.
"Go, prepare the troops," he said, "and have
Them standing ready by the hills of sand."
Zavāreh departed to assemble
The army at the battlefield. Rostam
Rode out, his lance in hand. When he passed through
The palace court, the army welcomed him
With eager shouts. "May horse and saddle, mace

---

* The monarch of China

And rope be never far from brave Rostam!"
He set off then, behind him Zavāreh,
His second in command. And so they rode
Until they reached the Hirmand's bank. The heart
Of Tahamtan was filled with sighs, his lips
With words of counsel he might speak. He left
The troops there, with Zavāreh, to ride alone
Toward the army of the shah. In private
He told his brother, "This man is base at heart
But has a demon's strength. I fear he'll be
Too much for me, and I'm unsure how this
Will end. You keep the army here. I'll go
And see what fate awaits us there. Although
He's angry, I won't send for warriors from
Zābolestān to come and fight with me,
But face him by myself. I would not have
A single man of ours be injured here.
Fortune favors the man who's just." He crossed
The river then, and climbed the bank upon
The farther side, still wondering at this turn
Of fate. He called, "O glorious Esfandiyār!
Prepare yourself to fight. Your enemy
Is here!" Esfandiyār, when he first heard
This challenge from Rostam, that aged and
Contentious lion, laughed and answered him,
"I've been prepared since I first woke, old man."
He ordered them to bring his helmet and
His armor, his quiver and his battle lance.
With these he clothed his radiant chest and arms,
And placed his royal helmet on his head.
The shah then bid them place a saddle on

His sable steed and bring him where he stood.
He buckled on his steel cuirass, and then
From joy, and from the strength he felt within
Himself, he thrust his lance's base into
The pitch-black earth, and like a leopard when
He pounces on an onager's bare back
To frighten it, he vaulted in his seat.
The soldiers were amazed at this, and praised
Their famous leader loud and long. He rode
Toward Rostam and saw him seated there,
Alone. Turning in his saddle, he said
To Pashutan, "I must not have a second
Or friend with me. Since he's alone, I'll fight
Alone as well. We'll ride from here below
Up to that crest." And so they went, the two
Of them, to war. It seemed as though all joy
And revelry had vanished from the earth.
As they approached the mountain crest, these two,
One young one old, both lionlike in pride
And strength, the cries of both their horses split
The air. It was as though the earth itself
Was rent in two. Rostam spoke first, his voice
Was hard: "O fortunate and happy shah,
Do not be obstinate in doing wrong.
Be wise instead, and seek what's fair and just.
If what you wish is war and bloodshed, the hard
And painful strife of men at arms, then say
So now, and I will bring you horsemen from
Zābol who've armed themselves with Kābol steel.
Here on this battlefield we'll have them fight,
While we stand by a while and watch. You'll see

Great tumult and confusion on all sides,
And blood enough to satisfy your wish."
Esfandiyār replied, "What has all this
To do with us? Today you rose at dawn,
Left home and palace, galloped here and led
Me to this mountain's crest. Why try to catch
Me now with tricks and lies? Perhaps you've seen
Your own decline lies just ahead. Why should
I wish to fight the people of Zābol
Or lead the army of Iran against
Kābol? To do so would not be my way.
Such actions are forbidden by my faith.
Nor would I shed Iranian blood like this
Or place a royal crown on my own head.
I will attack whoever comes to fight
With me, even if my challenger
Should be a warlike crocodile. If you
Require someone to fight beside you on
The field, I never have and never will.
In war my one companion is Yazdān.
And fortune smiles on everything I do.
You're eager for a fight, and so am I.
Let's face each other now without our troops.
We'll see whether Esfandiyār's horse returns
To feed at night without his rider or if
It is the steed of fierce Rostam who heads
With empty saddle to the palace stable."
The two agreed that in their combat none
Would interfere or act as rescuer.
First they attacked with lances. Blood poured from
Their coats of mail. They battled on until

Their lance tips broke, then of necessity
They drew their swords. Wheeling their horses right
And left, they thrust and parried skillfully.
At last, the fierceness of their horses' charge,
And of the blows that both the chieftains struck,
Shattered those heavy blades. Then, furious
As lions when they charge, they buffeted
Each other's bodies until the handles of
Their heavy maces broke. They paused in their
Attack, then firmly seized each other's belts.
Their swift-paced horses bent their necks as each
Man strained to lift the other from his seat,
But neither could be moved. Wearily,
They left the battleground, their horses both
Exhausted, too—mouths caked with dirt and blood,
Helmets dented, their armor slashed and torn.

TWO YOUTHS, TWO ROYAL PRINCES, LIE IN DUST (1055–1115)

The battle of the two great heroes had
Gone on for hours. When Rostam was delayed
Zavāreh grew troubled and brought his troops,
All keen to fight, toward the field. He called
To the Iranians, "Where is Rostam?
On such a day what can this silence mean?
You came here planning to make war on him,
To fight this famous crocodile, but you
Will never bind his hands, nor will we sit
Here idly as you try." He cursed them all,
Opening his lips to heap abuse and scorn
On all their chiefs. This angered Nush Āzar,

The son of Shah Esfandiyār, who was,
Though young, a fierce and skillful cavalier—
Both bold and resolute. Furious at
The insults of the hero from Sistān,
He cursed and swore at Zavāreh in turn,
And said, "It's true that noble warriors
Will do ignoble things, when ordered by
Their shah. But Shah Esfandiyār did not
Command that we should fight with dogs like you.
Who would ignore his orders? And who would dare
To break his pledge? If you, against all right,
Should challenge us and dare to meet us on
The battlefield, you'll see how warriors
Can fight with sword and lance and heavy mace."
Then Zavāreh commanded, "Draw your swords!
Place crowns of blood upon these chieftains' heads!"
Leading the army, Zavāreh advanced,
And sounds of battle rose above the field.
They slew countless Iranians, the sight
Of which enraged brave Nush Āzar. He armed
Himself, mounted his yellow steed, and with
An Indian sword in hand, he rode to war.
There was a famous hero, Alvā by name,
A proud, intrepid horseman, victorious
Upon the field, who carried Rostam's lance,
Protecting him from thrusts against his back.
Nush Āzar spied him across the field. He raced
Toward him, sword upraised, and struck him on
His head and shoulders, cleaving his body, huge
As any elephant's, from neck to waist.
Then Zavāreh, in turn, spurred his war-horse,

And called out angrily to Nush Āzar,
"Stand fast until I come! You've slaughtered brave
Alvā, a horseman without equal here."
With that he thrust his heavy lance and struck
The head of Nush Āzar into the dust.
When Nush Āzar, that famous prince, was killed,
The fortunes of the army perished, too.
His brother, Mehr-e Nush, a swordsman of
Renown, wept at this blow. Heart filled with grief,
Rage foaming at his lips, he spurred his huge
And mighty steed before the army's ranks,
While from the other side Farāmarz charged
Like a drunken elephant, his Indian sword
Upraised. He fell upon Mehr-e Nush as he
Advanced to meet his charge. The armies on
Both sides roared their support. These were two young
And precious warriors; one was a prince
By birth, the other one a pahlavān.
They battled with lionlike ferocity,
Raining blows upon each other's heads.
The anger of Mehr-e Nush was great, but on
The battlefield he lacked the strength to fight
With Farāmarz. One blow went wild and struck
His horse's neck, severing its head
And leaving him on foot. Then Farāmarz
Attacked him where he stood and struck him down;
Blood turned the battlefield to ruby red.
When Bahman saw his brother slain, the ground
Beneath his feet a mire of earth and gore,
He galloped to Esfandiyār and found
Him where the battle still raged fiery hot.

He said to him, "O fearsome lion chief,
The army of Sistān attacked us where
We stood and basely stole the lives of your
Two sons, Mehr-e Nush and Nush Āzar. You're in
The thick of battle, while we are filled with grief.
Two youths, two royal princes, lie in dust.
This shame, this work of fools, will stain our line
Forevermore." Rage waked the heart of Shah
Esfandiyār. Tears filled his eyes while wild
And stormy thoughts ran through his mind. He turned
And shouted at Rostam, "Oh, contemptible!
Is this how men of honor keep their word?
You swore, 'I will not bring my army to
The field.' You are unworthy of your name.
Are you not ashamed to stand before me or
To stand before your God? Do you not fear
The questions you'll be asked on Judgment Day?
Whoever breaks his word, as you have done,
Will not be praised by any man. Two of
Your heroes from Sistān have killed my sons
And still continue in their bloody rampage."
Rostam was deeply grieved by what he heard
And trembled like a willow branch. He swore
By sun and sword and battlefield, and by
The head of Shah Goshtāsp and his own soul,
"I did not order this attack, nor have
I words of praise for those who've done this deed.
I'll bind the hands of Zavāreh if he's
The one who led this fight. I'll bind as well
Both hands of Farāmarz and bring him to
Our pious shah. Slay both of them, and so

Avenge the blood of your two noble sons.
There let your anger at this madness end."
Esfandiyār replied, "To slay a snake
In vengeance for the murder of a peacock,
Who is the king of birds, would not be right,
Nor worthy of a proud and noble shah.
Ignoble wretch! Your time has come. Think how
To save yourself instead. With arrows from
This bow I'll stitch your thighs to Rakhsh's flanks
As close as milk and water in one cup.
When I am done, no slave will ever dare
To shed his master's blood. Should you survive,
I'll manacle your hand and carry you
At once to Goshtāsp's court." Rostam replied,
"What use is there to all these words except
To shame us more? Seek comfort and relief
In Him who guides us both in good and ill."

ARE YOU THE ONE WHO
MADE THE DEMONS WEEP? (1116–1198)

They grasped their deep curved bows and arrows made
Of poplar wood. Their fury dimmed the sun.
Sparks flashed from armor as the arrowheads
Stitched chain mail links to flesh. Esfandiyār
Grew furious at this. His face and brows
Were creased in rage. When he drew forth his bow
No one escaped his arrows. The world turned red
With blood; the bright sun hid its face in fear.
Esfandiyār uncased his tight strung bow—
It was as though the sun had cloaked its head.
His arrowheads were tipped with diamond points.

Both steel and paper were as one to them.
He loosed a hail of arrows from his bow
That pierced the bodies of Rostam and Rakhsh.
Huge Rakhsh was weakened by his wounds. Rostam
Grew faint as well. Esfandiyār pursued
Them without pause. The arrows of Rostam
Had no effect on him. Then swift as wind
Rostam dismounted from his saddle and raced
On foot toward the mountain's peak, while Rakhsh
The radiant parted from his lord and turned
Toward home. In that high place, the blood
So poured from Rostam's wounds that the Bisotun*
Of heroes trembled and grew weak. Below,
Esfandiyār the fortunate looked up
And laughed. "O famous Tahamtan," he said,
"This legendary strength of yours, like some
Mad elephant's, where is it now? Why have
My arrows pierced that elephantine hide?
Your mace and manly strength, your valor and
Pre-eminence in war, where are they now?
Why have you run away and scaled the heights?
Is it because you heard the lion's roar?
Is that what made the warlike elephant
Turn like a fox and flee the battlefield?
Are you the one who made the demons weep?
Is it your blade that singed the raging beasts?"
Suddenly, Zavāreh looked down and saw
The wounded Rakhsh making his way across
The stream. The world turned black before his eyes.
Lamenting loudly, he raced onto the field.
He saw his brother there, injured and bleeding,

---

* A mountain in western Iran

His wounds untended and undressed. He said,
"Get up. Take my horse, and flee! Should you
Be lost, who'll arm himself to seek revenge?"
Rostam replied to him, "Go, mount your horse,
And ride to Zāl. Tell him the glory of
The tribe of Sām has fled, and he must look
To remedy this loss. And who is there
To heal these wounds of mine? If I survive
The arrows of Esfandiyār, and live
'Til dawn, I know, Dastān, that here within
This company, I'll be like one reborn.
When you have gone, make healing Rakhsh your one
Concern. Though I'm delayed, I'll come at last."
Once Zavāreh had left his brother's side,
He rode in search of Rakhsh's trail. Below,
Esfandiyār delayed awhile, then called,
"Far-famed Rostam! How long do you intend
To stay up there? There's no one who can help
You now. Throw down your bow and tiger skin.
Unloose your sword and sword belt, too. If you'll
Repent and let your hands be bound, I swear
That you will suffer no further hurts from me.
I'll lead you, wounded, to the court and there
Excuse you of your crimes. But if you wish
To carry on this fight, then make your will.
Appoint someone to rule here in your place.
Ask God's forgiveness for your deeds. Perhaps
He'll generously accept your plea. Perhaps,
As well, he'll guide your steps once you have left
This transitory world." Rostam replied,
"Now's not the time for that. It's grown too late

For war and evil deeds. Who rides to battle
Once day has turned to night? It's time instead
For you to ride in triumph to your camp,
While I return like this toward home. I'll rest
Awhile and sleep, then bind up all my wounds.
I'll call those nearest me to counsel with—
Zāl, Farāmarz and Zavāreh—those of
My family who've gained renown. I'll do,
At last, whatever you command me to.
It's in your hands to choose what action's right."
Esfandiyār, the brazen-bodied,* said,
"O ancient, wilful rogue! I have observed
You in the fullness of your glory, and I've
No wish to see you in decline. I'll shield
Your soul for one more night. But when you've reached
Your home, do not attempt some clever ruse.
Do only that which you've agreed to do,
And after this, ask nothing more of me!"
Rostam agreed, "I'll do no more or less
Once I have found some way to remedy
These wounds." When he had parted from Rostam,
Esfandiyār observed him as he went.
He crossed the river like a ship, praying to
Yazdān to give his body strength. "O Lord
Of justice and of purity, if I
Should perish from these wounds, who will avenge
My name? Among these nobles, who has the courage
And sagacity to follow in my path?"
Esfandiyār looked on, as Rostam reached
The other bank and strode upon dry land.
"Do not call him a man," he said, "he is

---

* Zoroaster fed pomegranate seeds to Esfandiyār in order to render his
body invulnerable, or literally "brazen-bodied" (*ru'een tan*).

A huge, fierce elephant. He crossed the river
Despite the wounds that covered him, and crossed
It swiftly, too." In awe Esfandiyār
Exclaimed, "Almighty Judge, and Shaper of
Both Time and Place, You have created him
And made him as You wished." When he returned
Once more to camp, his brother, Pashutan,
Approached him from the palace tent. The air
Was filled with weeping and lamenting for
The heroes Nush Āzar and Mehr-e Nush.
Dust and ashes covered the royal tents,
The nobles all had torn their clothes in grief.
Esfandiyār dismounted from his steed.
He clasped the heads of those two gallants to
His side and said, "Farewell, my two brave youths,
Too soon your souls have fled your strong young bodies!"
He turned and said to Pashutan, "Rise up.
Don't weep too much for these two slain. I see
No benefit in shedding tears of blood.
Nor is it right to dwell too much on death.
We all are mortal, young and old alike.
May wisdom go with us when we depart."
In golden coffins and litters made of teak,
He sent them to his father, Shah Goshtāsp,
The lord of crown and throne. With them he sent
A message, too. "Your policy has borne
This fruit. You launched a boat into the stream
When you desired to make Rostam a slave.
Behold the bodies now of Mehr-e Nush
And Nush Āzar, and let the matter rest.
My future, like a calf still in the womb,

Is hidden from me. Who knows how this will end?"
Esfandiyār sat on his throne and grieved.
He pondered Rostam's words awhile, then spoke
To Pashutan: "The lion wisely flees
That man's fierce grip. Today I looked upon
The towering figure of Rostam—as huge
As any elephant—and praised the pure
Yazdān, our source of hope as well as fear,
Who made a man like this! All praise to the
Creator of the World! What wonders has
This Rostam done! He reached into the depths
Of China's sea to draw out crocodiles.
He brought the desert's leopards to his grasp
By simply drawing in his breath. And yet,
Today, I wounded him so deeply with
My arrows that the earth beneath his feet
Was soaked with blood. Although, with my consent,
He climbed down from the heights, his armor and
His sword upon his back, and waded to
The other bank, his wounds so weakened him—
Arrows pierced his body from head to foot—
That once he reaches home, I'm sure his soul
Will flee from there to heaven's highest sphere."

I HAVE ESCAPED THE DRAGON'S CLAWS (1199–1226)

While on the other side, Rostam at last
Reached home. His father, Zāl, beheld him in
This state. Both Zavāreh and Farāmarz
Were moved to tears, and grieved to see his wounds.
His mother, Rudābeh, plucked out her hair
And tore her face on hearing their laments.

Quickly, Zavāreh removed his belt
And tiger skin cuirass. The wise men of
The country, one and all, assembled in
The palace court, and took their seats. Rostam
Commanded them to lead Rakhsh in and bring
Him anyone who'd heal his wounds. Dastān,
The noble, tore his hair and pressed his cheeks
On Rostam's wounds. "That I, in my old age,
Should see my precious son in misery
Like this!" But Rostam said, "What use is there
In such laments? This comes from heaven and is
What's meant to be. The task before us now
Is far more difficult and weighs upon
My soul more heavily. However much
I strive to justify myself, and warm
The stony heart of this fierce lion, it seems
His only wish is to offend me more—
By words and deeds, and by his arrogance
And proud disdain. I've roamed the world from end
To end, confronted all its wonders and
Its mysteries as well. As lightly as
A willow branch, I seized the White Div by
His belt and threw him to the ground. And yet
I am not equal to Esfandiyār,
Not to his strength, nor to his gifts for war.
With my arrows I've pierced anvils and made light
Of shields. Today, I struck his armor with
Them many times. It mocked my archer's hand.
When leopards see my sword, they hide themselves
Behind a stone. It would not nick the mail
He wore upon his chest, nor even cut

The silken pennant on his helmet's crest.
I'm grateful to Yazdān for sending us
The night. Its darkness closed his eyes, so I
Escaped the dragon's claws. How can I know
If I'll escape these wounds as well? What can
I do? I see no other way than this:
At dawn I'll saddle Rakhsh and ride until
I reach some place he'll never find. If he,
In vengeance, should slaughter those within Zābol,
He'll tire of this at last, although it seems
He's slow to weary of such villainy."
Zāl answered him, "My son, listen to me!
And when you've heard me out, reflect on what
I say. In all this world there's only death
From which one can't escape, and death
Is an escape as well. I know a way
To save yourself. Choose it instead of flight.
I'll call upon Simorgh for help. If she
Will be my guide in this affair, we may
Remain as rulers of Zābolestān."

SADLY, SIMORGH DESCENDED FROM THE AIR (1227–1310)

Rostam agreed to this, and so Dastān
Set out to climb a lofty height. He brought
Three braziers filled with coals, and three alert
Companions went with him. The wizard, when
He reached the peak, drew out a feather from
A fine brocaded cloth. He raised a fire
Within a brazier, then burned a portion of
The feather in its flames. The first watch of
The night went by, then suddenly it seemed

The clouds turned iron black. From high above,
Simorgh looked down and saw the three hot fires,
And seated by their side the grief-struck Zāl.
Sadly, Simorgh descended from the air.
With fragrant aloes Zāl approached and praised
Her greatly, bowing low. As bloody tears
Coursed down his cheeks, he set three braziers there
Before her, and heaped them high with scented wood.
She said to him, "O shah! What has distressed
You so that you have called me with this smoke?"
He answered her, "May all the harm this base,
Ignoble wretch has brought on me fall on
My enemies as well! My son, Rostam,
The lion heart, is wounded; and since his wounds
Are mortal, I feel my soul in chains. No one
Has ever seen such wounds as these.
And Rakhsh is near to death as well. He writhes
In pain, his body pierced with arrowheads.
Esfandiyār came here not seeking either
A crown and throne, or land, but only war.
He would uproot this tree and crush its fruit."
Simorgh replied, "O pahlavān! Don't let
Misfortune crush your soul, but bring me Rakhsh,
And bring Rostam, that lord of all the world,
As well." Zāl sent a messenger to him.
"Rouse yourself, my son! Come to me now
In hope of being cured, and send at once
To have them fetch me Rakhsh as well." Rostam
Soon reached the height where that sagacious bird
Observed him well. "O fearsome elephant!"
She said. "Who's caused you such distress? Why did

You wish to fight Esfandiyār? Why choose
To burn yourself within his fire?" Zāl said
To her, "O Mistress of Benevolence,
Since you have shown us now your holy face,
Tell me, if Rostam's wounds cannot be healed,
What refuge is there left for me? To please
The warriors of Iran, they'll devastate
Sistān from end to end. They'll crush our seed,
Lay waste our house. What can we say, what must
We do?" Simorgh inspected Rostam's wounds
To find a way they could be cured. She drew
Four arrows out. Then with her beak, she sucked
Blood from them, too. At last, Simorgh pressed
A feather on his injured flesh, and he
Grew whole and sound. "Bind up your wounds," she said,
"And for a while avoid all injury.
Moisten a feather from my wing in milk,
And bind it on these wounds." In this same way
Simorgh called for Rakhsh, stretched out her beak to his
Right flank and plucked six arrows from his neck.
When she was done, no wounds or injuries
Remained. Rakhsh whinnied loudly and the Crown
Bestower laughed for joy. The great bird said,
"Huge-bodied hero! Renowned wherever men
Gather to speak of war! Why did you wish
To fight Esfandiyār? It is well known
He has a body hard as brass." Rostam
Replied, "It's only that he mentioned shackles.
The rest I could ignore. I'd rather face
My death than such a shame, even if death
Should come when I'm too weak to fight." "Surely,

To bow before Esfandiyār is no
Disgrace," she said. "In all the world, who is
His equal now? Iran can lift its head
Up high because of him. To hold back now
From fighting more would not seem strange but shrewd.
Be warned by my own case. With his sharp sword
And clever tricks he slew my mate, a bird
Of strength and majesty. If you will make
A pact with me right now and put aside
All thoughts of war with him, that is, if you
Won't try to best Esfandiyār in battle
Or on the field of war, and if his time
Should come, and he is slain, you vow you will
Not try to justify your crime, then I'll
Prepare a remedy, and you, once more,
May lift your head up to the sun." Rostam
Was overjoyed at her reply. He'd been
Released from fear of chains and fetters.
He said to her, "I will not disobey
Your words though sharpened swords rain down
Upon my head." Then Simorgh said, "Because
I love you, there's a secret I must tell
You now. Whoever sheds Esfandiyār's blood
Will be destroyed himself by fate. What's more,
So long as he shall live, misery
Will cling to him. While he's on earth he'll lead
A wretched life—unfortunate and poor—
And suffer more when he's passed on. I'll show
You miracles tonight and stop your lips
From speaking ill of him. Go now. Mount Rakhsh,
The shining, and choose a single, tempered blade."

Rostam put on his belt at her command,
And mounted Rakhsh from where he stood. "O Best
Of all the World," he said, "if I should die
Now, suddenly, what would it signify?
The world endures while we pass swiftly on,
And all we leave behind is what men say
Of us. It would be best that I should die
With my good name. My name must live because
My body's mortal. Where now are Feraydun
And Shah Hushang, who once possessed both throne
And crown? They've gone and left their places here,
For us. Such is the custom of the world."
He rode until he reached a lake. Simorgh
Appeared. The sky above his head grew dark.
As he approached the shore, the noble bird
Descended from the air. She pointed out
A path that led across dry land. The scent
Of musk arose from it. She brushed her wing
Across Tahamtan's brow, and ordered him
To come and stand before her there. He saw
A tamarisk growing nearby, its head
Raised to the sky, and there the royal bird
Alighted from the air. She said to him,
"Select a branch that's long and straight and slim.
Do not disdain this tamarisk. The death
Of brave Esfandiyār lies in its wood.
Straighten the branch over a fire. Choose one
Well-tried arrowhead to place upon its tip,
And feathers for its base. I've shown you now
How best to make it wound." Once Rostam had cut
A branch of tamarisk, he left the shore

And brought it to his home. Simorgh stood close
Beside him all the while to guide his work.
She said, "If now Esfandiyār should come
And challenge you to fight with him once more,
Appeal to him with peaceful, honest words.
Don't tread the path of trickery or try
Deceit. It may be that your gentle words
Will draw him back to sweeter speech himself.
Perhaps he will recall those times gone by,
The long and weary years that you have served
Iran's nobility. Should he reject
Your supplications, and treat you as a man
Of little worth, then string your bow and take
This arrow made of tamarisk, which first
You'll soak in wine, and then, with both your hands,
Send it straight toward his eyes, as those who worship
The tamarisk would do. Your rage and fate
Together will bear that fateful tamarisk
Directly to his eyes." Simorgh embraced
Dastān, weaving their bodies close as warp
And woof, and said good-by. Content, she then
Flew off. When Rostam saw her rising up
Into the air, he lit a blazing fire,
Delighted at the coming strife. Then to
The shaft he fixed a sharpened arrowhead,
And right and left, bound feathers to the haft.

WORLDLY WEAPONS WOULD
NEVER SERVE HIM NOW (1311–1364)

Sunlit dawn galloped from the mountains
And pranced among the fields of night. Rostam

Took up his weapons, reciting as he did
A prayer to the Maker of the World.
He rode toward the army of Iran,
With vengeance in his heart. As he approached
His famous foe, he called to him, "Wake up
Esfandiyār from your sweet sleep! Time now
To face Rostam, who's eager for revenge."
Esfandiyār heard Rostam's voice and knew
That worldly weapons would never serve him now.
To Pashutan he said, "The lion will turn
And flee this warrior's grip. I did not think
Rostam would ever reach his home again
With helmet, armor and his tiger skin.
The same for Rakhsh, who bears him to the field.
His body's free of arrows now. I'd heard
That Zāl knew sorcery and could, at will,
Draw strength down from the sun. That he,
When in a rage, was far more powerful
Than others of this craft. I doubted this.
It made no sense to me." Tears filled the eyes
Of Pashutan as he replied to him,
"May grief and rage afflict your enemies.
What's happened that you lack all vigor and
Resolve today? Did you not sleep last night?
What in the world has happened to this pair
Of valiant men that they must suffer so?
I know your fortune has begun to fail
Because, once more, it leads you on to war."
The hero Esfandiyār put on his shirt
Of mail, mounted his horse and rode toward
His famous foe. When he could see his face,

He cried, "May your name vanish from the earth!
You, from Sistān, have you forgotten what
Your enemy's fierce arm and bow can do?
The clever tricks of Zāl have healed your wounds,
Or else you would be lying in a grave.
Today I will so batter you that Zāl
Will never again see you alive." Rostam
Replied, "I see that you, Esfandiyār,
Are still not weary of this strife. Fear Pure Yazdān,
The Maker of the World. Don't hide your heart
And wisdom in some pit. Today I've come
To plead for pardon and my honor, not
To fight with you. Your quarrel with me is
Unjust, because you close your eyes to what
Is wise and true. By Zand Avesta and
By sun and moon, I beg you, don't pursue
This path that ends in loss. Do not recall
The words that we have spoken here, 'though they
Were harsh enough to split your skin. Come visit me
Within my home. Desire to please you fills
My heart. I'll open wide the doors of all
My ancient treasuries, those I've amassed
Through many years, and load their contents on
The backs of my own beasts. These you may give
Your treasurer to drive before us on
The road. I'll ride beside you as we go,
And when we reach the royal court, I'll do
Whatever you may ask of me. If I
Am culpable, and he should have me slain,
That would be right. The same if he commands
That I be bound. I'll do this so that fate,

At last, may sate you with the love of war.
Recall this saying of some ancient sage,
'An evil star should never be one's mate.'"
He answered him, "Why must you chatter so
About your home and treasury, and why
Put on for me the shining face of peace?
I won't be fooled by clever words when war
Or danger threatens. If you would stay alive
Don't speak. Put shackles on your feet instead."
Once more Rostam unloosed his tongue, "Do not,
O shah, speak so unjustly yet again.
Don't shame my name before the world. Nothing
But bad will come of such an evil act.
I'll give you now a thousand royal jewels,
Golden earrings and bracelets, too. I'll send
A thousand sweet-lipped slaves who'll serve you day
And night, a thousand serving maids as well,
Each one from Khallokhi and radiant as
A gem. What's more, O shah without compare,
I'll open up the treasuries of Sām
And Zāl and Narimān, and heap them up
Before your throne. I'll bring you soldiers from
Zābolestān, who'll pledge their souls to your
Command, who will obey your every word.
And then, just like a slave, I'll gallop with
You to Shah Goshtāsp's court. O Shahriyār!
Put thoughts of vengeance from your heart! Don't yoke
Your wisdom to a demon's wish. You are
A shah, a pious man, you've other means
Than bonds to show your strength. Use them on me.
To wear these bonds will shame my name for all

Eternity and injure you as well."
Esfandiyār replied to Rostam's plea,
"How long will you go on like this? You tell
Me 'Turn aside from Yazdān's path, ignore
The shah's commands!' The shah is keeper of
The world. Whoever disobeys the shah
Will quickly meet with death. Answer me
With bonds or with a call to fight. Do not
Reply in any other way." Rostam,
The famous warrior, spoke then in anger,
"O, worthy shah, you slight my words and wish
To injure me, not knowing what you do."
"Enough of such deceits," he answered him,
"Disaster presses hot against your back!"

HIS BODY, TALL AND STRAIGHT...
BENT TO THE EARTH (1365–1441)

Rostam knew that now it would be fruitless
To reason further with Esfandiyār.
He strung his bow and grasped the arrow made
Of tamarisk, whose point he'd cured in wine.
He placed it on the bow, then turned his face
Toward the sky. "O God, Creator of
The sun! Pure Lord of wisdom, strength
And majesty. You see my unstained soul,
My strength and my integrity, and how
I've bent and twisted so Esfandiyār
Would turn aside from war at last.
You know his actions are unjust. You see
Him taunt me with his virtue and his strength,
And challenge me to fight. O creator of

The moon and mercury, don't punish me
For my grave sin!" Because Rostam
Was slow to fight, the headstrong warrior
Called out to him, "Come, my deceitful foe,
I see that your Sistānian soul has lost
Its taste for war! But now, you must confront
The arrowheads of Shah Lohrāsp, the shafts
Of Shah Goshtāsp and my own lion heart!"
Then, with all the force of his great bow,
He shot an arrow that struck the helmet of
Rostam. As Simorgh had instructed him,
Tahamtan quickly placed the arrow made
Of tamarisk upon his bow and struck
Esfandiyār's eyes with it. The world grew black
Before him. Wisdom and glory fled. The head
Of that great shah, who'd served Yazdān so well,
Drooped to his chest. His body, tall and straight
As any cypress tree, bent to the earth.
His hardwood bow slipped from his grasp. He clutched
His horse's mane and chest as the earth beneath
Turned ruby red. Tahamtan said, "You've brought
This bitter seed to fruit. You were the one
Who said, 'My body's made of brass! Heaven
Is not so high I cannot pluck it down.'
Eight times you struck my body with your arrows.
No shameful sigh escaped my lips. But now,
A single arrow has ended your attack
And left you prostrate on your horse. Soon,
Your head will touch the earth, and soon, the heart
Of Katāyun will burn with grief." Just then
The famous shah fell headlong from his horse.

For a moment he lay still, then consciousness
Returned, and he sat up, listening
To hear who'd come. He grasped the arrow firmly
And plucked it out—its shaft and feathers drenched
In blood. Meanwhile, word reached Bahman that now
The glory of the shāhanshāh was dimmed.
He went to Pashutan, and said, "This war
Of ours has ended in great misery.
The body of that warlike elephant
Lies in the dust, and all our hearts are shattered
By pain and grief." The two of them ran from
The army to the battlefield and saw
The pahlavān, his chest all smeared with gore,
A bloody arrow in his hand. Weeping
Loudly, Pashutan tore his clothes
And threw dark dust upon his head. Bahman
Writhed in the dirt and pressed his cheek against
His father's bloody chest. While Pashutan
Lamented, "Who among the priests and nobles
Can understand the riddle of this world?
Why should a hero, who like Esfandiyār
Bravely unsheathed his sword to serve his faith,
Who purged idolaters from all the world—
Their villainy with them—and was himself
Quite guiltless of all wrong, be struck down in
His youth, and lay his head, so worthy of
A crown, upon the earth? The wicked man,
Who's caused the world great suffering and racked
The souls of noble men, enjoys a long
And peaceful life, and never looks upon
The misery of war." Some youths approached

To lift Esfandiyār's body from the earth
And wipe it clean of gore. His brother's face
Was wet with bloody tears, his heart suffused
With anguish, as he lamented over him.
"Valiant Esfandiyār," he cried, "the seed
Of noble stock and lord of all the world.
Who's overthrown this warlike mountain peak?
Who's wrenched the tusk out of the elephant's jaw?
Who's filled the river Nile with waves of weeping?
Who's thrown the charging lion to the earth?
Why has the evil eye so scowled upon
Our family? Surely, immoral acts
Alone bring on such evil ends. Where are
Your matchless skills in war; where is your sweet,
Melodious voice at feasts? Where have they gone,
Your courage, wit and charm; your faith, your strength,
Your lucky star? Because you cleansed the earth
Of sinful men and feared no elephant
Or lion, you've earned a just reward. But now,
Instead, your fate awaits you in the grave.
Curses on this crown and throne, and on
This endless struggle and this crooked fate!
When a brave and youthful cavalier, who is
Renowned for skill and wisdom, is slain upon
The battlefield like this, and all his days
On earth are ended here in weeping, I say
Let there be no more crown or throne! No Shah
Goshtāsp, no sage Jāmāsp, no splendid court!"
The wise Esfandiyār replied to him,
"O happy and sagacious man! Don't slay
Yourself because of me! This is the crown

And throne that was my fate. My body has
Been slain, and it will rest in earth. You need
Not mourn my death. Where now are Feraydun,
Hushang and Jam? The wind that brought them here
Has carried them away—our ancestors,
Those proud and pure-born chiefs, as well. They've gone,
And left their places here for us. This is
A caravansary; none stays here long.
I've labored in the world for many years,
Both publicly and privately, to serve
The cause of Yazdān's faith and make wise thought
The guide to true belief. When my labors for
Enlightenment took hold and blocked the path
Of evil Ahriman, fate reached for me
With knifelike claws, from which time left me no
Escape. My hope is that in paradise
My heart and soul will harvest what they've sown.
Although the son of Zāl has slain me now,
It wasn't by his strength and skill. Look at
This arrow made of tamarisk. My days
On earth were ended by this piece of wood.
This, and Simorgh, and clever Tahamtan.
Zāl wove the sorcery. He's master of
The earth's deceits and treacheries." He spoke,
And Rostam writhed in agony, and wept.
"Some ill-intentioned div incited you
To bring misfortune on me now, he thought.
To those assembled there he said, "It was
Exactly as he's said. He is a man
Of virtue and does not deviate from truth.
Since I first armed myself for war, I've fought

With many proud and skillful warriors.
There is no horseman like Esfandiyār.
Not one can equal him among all those
Who arm themselves with helmet and cuirass.
When, in despair, I fled from him, knowing
I could not face his bowman's mighty chest
And fist, I saw my only hope lay in
This stratagem and yielded wholly to it.
I placed this fateful arrow on my bow,
And when his hour had come, I shot it in
His eye. If he were given back his life,
Would bow or tamarisk avail me then?
We all must leave this dusky earth. Take heed!
We cannot draw one breath beyond our time.
I was the agent of the tamarisk; that's all.
I am what's dark and dismal in this tale."

THIS WRONG WAS DONE TO ME BY GOSHTĀSP SHAH! (1442–1517)

Esfandiyār addressed Rostam and said,
"My days have reached their end. Don't flee from me.
Rise up, come near. My thoughts toward you now
Are not the same as they once were. If you
Will hear my counsel and advice, you'll know
Me better and come to understand my worth.
Make use of my advice, be guided by
Your noble heart in this." Rostam agreed
To his request. Lamenting, he approached
Esfandiyār on foot. Hot tears poured from
His eyes, and doleful sighs escaped his lips.
Zāl learned the news, and swift as wind, he left

The palace, racing toward the battlefield.
As he approached the place where they had fought,
Tears filled his eyes, and anguish seared his heart.
Zavāreh and Farāmarz, like men
Lost in a daze, galloped toward the field
With several of their guard. A cry rose up
That dimmed the sun and moon. Zāl turned
To Tahamtan and said, "My son, my heart
Grieves more for you. I've heard a Chinese sage
And wise astrologers from Goshtāsp's court
Say this, 'Whoever sheds Esfandiyār's blood
Will shortly die himself. Within
This world, dark misery will dog his steps,
And when he passes on he'll suffer more.'"
Esfandiyār addressed Rostam,
"What I've endured comes from the times, not you.
My fate has been as it was meant to be.
Take heed of what I say. I have been harmed
By Goshtāsp's wicked dreams, not by this bow
And arrow, nor by Simorgh and Tahamtan.
He said, 'Go, burn Sistān. From this day on
Nimruz shall cease to be. That is my wish.'
He sent me off to war so he'd enjoy
His army, crown, and treasury in peace.
Here is Bahman, my famous son, my wise,
Alert vizier; when I shall die, treat him
As though you were his father, and take to heart
These things I'll tell you now. Keep him with you
Here in Zābolestān, and cheer his heart.
Teach him to know dishonest speech. Instruct
Him in the arts of war, the etiquette

Of feasting, hunting and the playing field,
The manners of the court, the uses of
Authority, and how best to spend his time.
Jāmāsp, whose name I curse, once said that in
This world I'd always fail of my desire.
But that Bahman would keep my name alive
And live to be a greater shah than I."
Rostam stood up and struck his chest with his
Right arm to show that he assented to
Esfandiyār's command. "When you have gone
I will not fail of this bequest but strive
To see that it's fulfilled in every way.
I'll seat him on the famous ivory throne,
And place the much-prized crown upon his head."
When he had heard Rostam's reply, he said,
"Accept what's new. The old has passed away.
As Yazdān is my witness, and guides me to
The Best of Faiths, know this, despite the good
That you have done, despite how you have served
The shahs of times long past, your worthy name
Will now be cursed as all the world laments
The passing of Esfandiyār. Great pain
Will now afflict your soul. This is your fate,
As He who made the world decrees." He turned
And spoke to Pashutan: "There's nothing that
I ask the world for now, except a shroud.
When I have left this transitory realm,
Gather our troops, and lead them to Iran.
Once there, say to my father, 'Since now, at last,
You've reached the goal you sought, make no
Pretense of grief. The times are now as you

Long wished they'd be. Your name fills all the land.
It's not what I had hoped from you, but this
Best suits your pitch-black soul. I wielded
The sword of justice and set the world to rights.
None dared to threaten Shah Goshtāsp. And when
The Best of Faiths had triumphed in Iran,
Greatness and kingship beckoned me. Before
The nobles of the court, you honored me,
But secretly you sent me to my death.
You've gained your heart's desire from this affair.
Prepare to celebrate and take your ease.
Your throne's secure; drive thoughts of death away.
Prepare a feast within the royal court.
You have the throne; I have the pain. You have
Renown, and I, a grave and winding sheet.
But don't rely too much on army, throne
And treasury. What was it that the wise
Old _dehqān_* said? "No arrow outshoots death."
My soul will wait for you beside the road.
Once you've arrived, we'll go, the two of us,
To face the Judge of All. We'll state our case
And hear what He decides.' From Goshtāsp go
To seek my mother, and tell her this from me,
'The warrior has had enough of war—
He whose arrows would fly through hills of steel
And before which armor was like air. Follow
Me quickly, dear one. Don't trouble yourself,
Nor grieve your soul for me. Don't bare your face
Before the court, nor look upon my own
When I am in my shroud. Seeing my face
Will make you weep too much, which none among

---

* Small landholder. A repositories of traditional Iranian culture

The wise will praise. So also, my sisters and
My wife, those wise and skillful women, who shared
My home. Say my farewell to them for all
Eternity. My father's crown has heaped
Misfortune on my head. He thought my soul
The key to what he valued most. I send
It to him now to make his own feel shame.'"
He paused, took one last breath and said, "This wrong
Was done to me by Goshtāsp Shah!" Just at
That instant, his pure soul left his wounded body,
And he collapsed upon the dusky earth.
Rostam drew near to Pashutan, the clothes
Upon his body rent from head to foot.
Dust covered both his head and brow. Pain filled
His heart. He said, lamenting, as he spoke,
"Farewell, great cavalier, the grandson of
The valiant Lohrāsp, and son to Shah
Goshtāsp. My name was known for virtue once.
But through Goshtāsp my fame has turned to dust."
He wept and sighed, then spoke once more to slain
Esfandiyār. "You were a shah who had
No equal in the world. I pray your soul
Is now in heaven and that your enemy
Will reap what he has sown." Then Zavāreh
Addressed him to admonish him: "Do not
Accept this trust," he said. "The dehqāns give
Us shrewd advice on this, which you should heed.
If you would raise a lion cub, be warned
That when his teeth are sharp, and he's full grown,
He'll surely seek for prey. The one he'll first attack
Is he who nourished him. Once death has freed

These heroes from the evil eye, Zābol
Will be the first to suffer harm. When a shah
Like brave Esfandiyār's been killed, we'll see
The worst of times. Some injury will come
To us from Bahman's hand. The ancients of
Kābol will suffer, too. When Bahman sits
Upon the throne, he'll take revenge for Shah
Esfandiyār's death." Rostam replied, "Whether
For good or ill, there's none who has the strength
To outmatch fate. I choose to do that which
Seems wise to me, and brings new honor, too.
If he should choose to do us harm, it's he
Who flouts the age, and it will turn on him.
Do not be quick to scratch misfortune's eye."

THIS LAND WILL NEVER SEE YOUR LIKE AGAIN! (1518–1602)

A splendid iron coffin was made for him
And lined with Chinese silk. The sides were sealed
With pitch, on which they sprinkled sandalwood,
Musk and fragrant herbs. His winding sheet
Was made of gold brocade. The famous lords
Assembled by his bier and wept. And after,
They clothed his glorious body and set a crown
Of turquoise on his head, then firmly closed
The lid upon his narrow coffin. So passed
Away that fruitful, royal tree. Rostam
Chose forty camels from the best he had,
And these he draped with fine brocade. Two carried
The coffin of the shah. Left and right,
And front and back, the army marched with them.
Faces bloody, their hair torn out in hanks,

They called his name, longing to see his face.
At the army's head rode Pashutan, who led
His pitch-black horse, its mane and tail cut short,
Its saddle front to back. Esfandiyār's mace
Hung from the saddle tree together with
His warrior's helmet and mailed shirt, his bow
And quiver, too. The army marched away
While Bahman stayed behind. His cheeks ran wet
With bloody tears. Tahamtan led him to
His royal home and cared for him as though
He were his soul. News reached Goshtāsp from those
Still on the road, "The famous shah has been
Brought low." He tore his clothes, cast off his crown
And flung himself upon the ground. A clamor
Of mourning arose within the court and palace;
Cries of "Esfandiyār" filled all the world.
Throughout Iran, whoever heard the news
Despaired, and threw his crown into the dirt.
Goshtāsp exclaimed, "O pure of faith, this land
Will never see your like again! Down from
The time of Manuchehr to our own day,
There's never been a prouder chief than you.
He bloodied his sword to purify the faith,
And he restrained our noble chiefs as well."*
Iran's great lords grew angry with the shah
And, weeping, cleansed their eyes of reverence
For him. They all cried out, "Unfortunate
And bitter man! To keep your throne you sent
One like Esfandiyār to face Rostam—
Consigning him to death—then placed the crown
Of the Kayānid line† on your own head.

---

* These lines are spoken as an aside.
† A dynasty founded by Kay Qobād

129

May that great crown bring shame to you, and may
It slow your star's ascent as well." With one
Accord they left Goshtāsp. Dust filled the court
And palace of Iran. His mother and
His sisters heard the news and left the palace
Together with their daughters. Their heads and feet
Were bare; dust covered them. The clothes upon
Their bodies hung in rags. As Pashutan
Approached the court, he wept, following behind
The coffin and black horse. The women clung
To him as tears of blood poured from their eyes.
"Undo the coffin's lid," they begged, "so we
May see his wounded body one last time."
With anguished women surrounding him, the grief-
Struck Pashutan, who sobbed and tore the flesh
Upon his arms, called to the blacksmiths, "Come,
And bring sharp files! Today is Judgment Day."
They lifted off the coffin's narrow lid,
And lamentation started up anew.
When they had seen his face, his fine black beard
Perfumed with musk, his mother and his sisters
All left their loved one's pillow and went to where
His sable horse was standing. They tenderly
Caressed its mane and chest. Then Katāyun
Scattered its body with dark dust because
This was the horse on whom the fortune of
Esfandiyār had turned. He had been killed
While riding him. "And now, what hero will
You carry off to war? Whom will you thrust
Into the dragon's claws?" They hung upon
His mane and poured dark dust upon his brow.

The army's sighs and groans rose to the clouds.
When Pashutan approached the palace of
Goshtāsp, he shouted once in greeting but did
Not bow to honor him. He strode up to
His throne, and said, "O chief of all who rule,
Fortune has turned its back on you. The proof
Of that is here. It's you who struck this blow
Against yourself and stirred up enmity
Within Iran. Wisdom and royal grace
Have fled from you. The punishment of God
Is what you'll find instead. The prop that held
You up is shattered now. What's left is wind
Within your hand. To keep your throne you gave
Your son away to death. But now your eyes
Will neither see the throne nor look upon
A rising star. Your enemies, and men
Who'll do you harm, fill all the world.
The crown won't stay with you, no, not for long.
While you still live, you'll suffer harsh rebukes
And face the Lord of All on Judgment Day."
When he was done, he turned to face Jāmāsp.
"You are an evil man, ungodly and
Base born," he said. "Your speech is lies, and with
Your cunning tongue, you steal men's light. You set
The Kays to feuding, in private turning each
Against the other. What do you teach except
The vilest things—how to avoid the right
And gather in the wrong. You've sown your seeds.
Now you will harvest them, both in the court
And privately. Your words have slain this great
And noble man, and with him dies the hope

Of all nobility. You aged, hunchbacked dwarf!
You taught the shah to walk this crooked path!
You said to him, 'Your son Esfandiyār's life
Lies in the palm of Rostam's hand.'" He paused,
Then spoke again, and eloquently retold
For them the wisdom and advice he'd heard—
The counsels of Bahman, and Rostam, too.
What had been hidden he made known, and told
These secrets boldly to Goshtāsp, who ruled
The world. The shah, on hearing this, felt shame
At what he'd done to brave Esfandiyār.
When court and palace had been emptied of
Iran's nobility, Homay and Beh Afrid,
The sisters of Esfandiyār, entered
And stood before the shah, tearing their cheeks
And hair in mourning for their brother's death.
They cried, "O famous shah! Haven't you thought
Of what Esfandiyār's death will mean for you?
After Zarir was slain, he was the first
To seek revenge against the Turks and snatched
The lion's prey from right between its paws.
He placed your monarchy on solid ground.
Yet on the word of one who wished him ill
You had him bound with heavy ropes and chains.
While he was bound, Lohrāsp was slain, and fortune
Abandoned the legions of Iran and you.
From Chinese Turkestān Arjāsp advanced
To Balkh. Our lives grew difficult and harsh.
We, who wear the veil, and live at court,
Were driven naked through the streets. At Nush
Āzar, he quenched the flame that Zarātosht

First lit.* And next he seized the monarchy
Of all Iran. You know as well as we
What your brave son did then. He crushed
The army of Arjāsp, returned us from
The Brazen Fort to you, secured your crown
And served as guardian for all Iran.
From here, you sent him to Zābol, but first
You gave him shrewd advice and learned counsel,
So that to serve the crown he'd lose his life
And all the world be driven mad with grief.
Not by Simorgh, nor by Rostam or Zāl,
Was your son slain. You murdered him. Since it
Was you who took his life, do not lament
And sigh. Your white beard shames you now. You killed
Your son to satisfy your greed. There have
'Til now been many shahs, each worthy of
The throne he sat upon. None killed his son.
None killed the children of his family."
Goshtāsp turned then to Pashutan, "Go now
And try to quench this burning flame." He left
The palace grounds, leading the women of
The court. He asked his mother, Katāyun,
"How long will you still grieve and beat your fists
Against this narrow door? His rest is calm;
His soul at peace. He had grown weary of
This court and of its lord." At last the queen
Took in the solace of her pious son
And was contented with the justice of
The Judge of All. Each year from that day on,
Cries of grief and lamentation filled
All temples in Iran. They sorrowed for

---

* Here, "Nush Āzar" is the name of a Zoroastrian fire temple, not the son
of Esfandiyār.

That fateful arrow made of tamarisk
And for the wily stratagems of Zāl.

THE STORY OF ESFANDIYĀR
HAS REACHED ITS END (1603–1666)

In Zābol Bahman's days were spent meanwhile
In court and garden, and the hunt. Rostam
Instructed him in courtly etiquette,
In feasting, drinking and fine horsemanship.
This royal prince he treated as his son
In everything, and kept him cheerful day
And night. When he'd made good upon his word,
And closed the door against Goshtāsp's revenge,
He wrote a letter to the shah in which
He painfully retold the story of
His son. At first he offered praise to those
Who felt no enmity, nor sought revenge.
Then said, "Izad and Pashutan are both
My witnesses. I begged Esfandiyār,
Time after time, to put aside all thoughts
Of war and strife. I offered him my lands
And treasury. I said I would accept
Whatever punishment was mine. But this
Was not to be. Fate did not smile on him.
My heart is filled with pain, my thoughts with love.
The sky turns as it will, and time is far
Too strong for any man. Bahman, his bold
Ambitious son, is here with me. He is
A noble youth and my propitious star.
I've taught him how to be a shāhanshāh,
Instructing him as wisdom guided me.

If the shah, who pardons penitents, will swear
To put that arrow from his thoughts, then I
Am his in soul and body. My lands and wealth,
My very flesh and bones, are his as well."
When Rostam's letter reached the shah, he had
It shown to all the nobles of the court.
Then Pashutan approached and testified
To all Rostam had said. He told him of
His grief, his counsel and appeal, and of
The offer of his lands and fealty.
The shah was happy with his famous son.
Some good would come of this appeal. His heart
Was softened toward Rostam; it burned with grief
No more. He wrote at once to answer him,
Planting a tree within the garden of
His majesty. "When, in its tyranny,
High heaven will do a man some harm, how can
He hold it back by either learning or
By flight? I've learned from Pashutan what your
Intentions were, and I am pleased by this.
The turning heavens will not pause for us,
Nor does a wise man linger on the past.
You are what you have been, and more. You are
The lord of Hendustān and of Ghannuj.
Whatever more you'd have—a signet ring,
A throne, a sword, a helmet—it shall be yours."
The messenger brought back the shah's reply
At once, just as Rostam had ordered him.
Some time went by like this, until the prince
Had grown to his full height. In knowledge, strength
And wisdom, he now was worthy of a crown.

Jāmāsp was sure that sovereignty, for good
Or ill, would be Bahman's at last. He told
Goshtāsp, "O worthy shah! Consider well
Your grandson, Prince Bahman. You'll find in him
The learning that his father wished for him.
He has matured into a man of worth
And probity. For many years he's lived
Far from Iran, and no one's read to him
A letter sent by you. Write to him now,
A letter like a tree in Paradise.
Who else, in all the world, was left you by
Esfandiyār to ease your sorrow at
His death?" These words were welcome to the shah.
He told the fortunate Jāmāsp, "Write this
Reply to fierce and proud Rostam from me,
'Yazdān be thanked, great pahlavān, who cheers
Our heart and lifts our spirit! Bahman, our grandson,
Who's dearer to us than our soul, and who
Is better known for wisdom than Jāmāsp,
Has, through your auspices, acquired both skill
And judgment. It's time that he return to us.'
And send this letter to Bahman as well,
'Once you have read this letter, leave Zābol.
We long to see you here. Prepare yourself
To come. Do not delay.'" When the scribe had read
This letter to Rostam, his heart rejoiced.
He chose fine gifts from what he had within
His treasury—mailed shirts and tempered blades
From India, maces, bows and arrows,
Armor; and camphor, musk, fresh ambergris,
And aloe wood; gold, silver, precious gems,

Fleet horses, bolts of uncut cloth; female slaves,
Both children and full grown, golden stirrups
And bridles, two ruby goblets inlaid with gold
As well—all these he gave Bahman. They all
Were listed in his treasury by those
Who carried them. Rostam accompanied
Bahman two stages on the road, then sent
Him to the shah. When Goshtāsp looked upon
His grandson's face his cheeks were drenched with tears.
He said, "You are Esfandiyār himself.
I find no trace of any other man
In you." He saw he was alert and quick to learn,
So from that time he called him Ardashir.
He was a warrior, with powerful arms,
Learned, wise and faithful to Yazdān.
Erect, his arms extended to his knees.
They tested him in fighting, feasting and
The hunt for several days. In all of these,
And on the polo field as well, he was
The equal of Esfandiyār. Goshtāsp
Did not grow weary of his company,
And when he called for wine, he looked on him
With doting eyes. "You are a gift to me
From God, a consolation in my grief.
Bahman will stay with me forevermore,
Because my brave Esfandiyār is gone."

*　　*　　*

The story of Esfandiyār has reached
Its end at last. Long may the shahriyār live!
His heart forever freed of care, the times
Obedient to his command. May he
Rejoice upon his famous throne, a rope
Around the necks of those who wish him ill.

Translator's Afterword

No elaborate justification seems necessary for undertaking a new translation from a classic work; particularly when, like the *Shahnameh*, it has been neglected for so long. The only complete poetic translation of the *Shahnameh* into English, that of Arthur George Warner and Edmond Warner, was completed in 1925 (*The Shahnama of Firdausi*. 9 vols. London: 1905–25). Although this translation can still be consulted to advantage, the Warners' English now seems dated, their work was based on late and corrupt manuscripts and all nine volumes are long out of print. Since then the only new English translation that attempts to include the whole work is the prose paraphrase by Reuben Levy (Chicago: 1967). Levy leaves out large portions of the text, especially those passages that focus on the ethical and moral issues that are central to Ferdowsi's genius, and he gives undue emphasis to martial prowess and royal splendor. Levy's work also appeared before the publication of better editions based on earlier manuscripts—specifically those of Ye. E. Bertel, et al.(Moscow: 1960–71), and Djalal Khaleghi-Motlagh (Costa Mesa, California and New York: 1987–).

In the last twelve years two individual tales have been translated into English blank verse: my own, *The Tragedy of Sohrab and Rostam* (1987), and Dick Davis's *The Legend of Seyavash* (1992). These translations bring Ferdowsi's poetry to modern audiences in a language closer to their own, and they more accurately represent the poem as he composed it. Sohrab and Seyavash are the first two of a triumvirate of stories that modern readers generally agree are the most remarkable and compelling of Ferdowsi's creations. The third is Rostam and Esfandiyar, and some critics, myself included, would argue that it is the most powerful of the three. It is a leaner work, a drama of words more than actions, with a limited cast of characters, whose focus is the moral dilemma that both unites and destroys its two heroes. It is as though Ferdowsi chose to clear away all that was extraneous to this central drama in order to develop it more fully. I have again chosen to translate Ferdowsi's couplets into blank verse, long the vehicle of choice for rendering epic into English. I have also used a somewhat freer line than I did in Sohrab in order to capture more fluently the mounting psychological tension that underlies the lengthy, complex dialogue between the two protagonists.

She'ar and Anvari's edition of *Rostam and Esfandiyar* is based on the British Museum manuscript of 1276–7, as are both scholarly editions mentioned above. It has the additional advantage for the student and translator of extensive explanatory annotations that draw on a wide range of current scholarship in Persian. In making my own translation I have consulted both the Warners' English translation and Jules Mohl's monumental rendering into French (Paris: 1838–78; reprint 1976). Those wishing to learn more about Ferdowsi and his great work could not do better than to begin with Dick Davis's masterly study, *Epic and Sedition: The Case of the Shahnameh* (Fayetteville, Arkansas: 1992). The relation of Ferdowsi's work to the oral tradition is discussed in Olga Davidson's important work, *Poet and Hero in the Persian Book of Kings* (Ithaca, New York: 1994).

For more general information about the Persian literary tradition there are a number of literary histories of Iran, or Persia, in English. See, for example, those by A. J. Arberry (London: 1958), Jan Rypka, et. al., (Dordrecht, Holland: 1968), or, most recently E. Yarshater, et. al., (1988). Finally, Dick Davis is preparing a beautifully illustrated prose retelling of the whole of the *Shahnameh* in three volumes. The first of these, *The Lion and the Throne*, is now in print, and the second, *Fathers and Sons* is scheduled to appear in late 1999 (Washington, DC: 1997–).

About the Translator

Jerome W. Clinton was born in San Jose, California, in 1937. He studied English and American literature at Stanford (A.B.) and at the University of Pennsylvania (M.A.), before two years in Iran with the Peace Corps redirected his interest to Persian. He received his Ph.D. in Persian and Arabic literature from the University of Michigan in 1972. Since then he has taught at the University of Minnesota and, since 1974, at Princeton University. Prior to moving to Princeton he directed the Tehran Center of the American Institute of Iranian Studies for two years. He is the author of a textbook, *Modern Persian: Spoken and Written* (with Donald L. Stilo), a monograph of the eleventh-century Persian poet Manuchehri Damghani, and briefer studies and translations from modern and classical Persian.